THE TIMOTHY INITIATIVE

Book 2
Communicating the Bible

Revised

This book belongs to:

_____

18.07.2019

"And the things you have heard from me among many witnesses, commit these to faithful men who will be able to teach others also."

2 Timothy 2:2

TTI Contact Information:

admin@ttionline.org

TTI Website:

www.ttionline.org

Book 2
Communicating the Bible
This edition published by The Timothy Initiative

All rights reserved.

Scripture quotations are from: The New King James Version
Copyright © 1979, 1980, 1982 by Thomas Nelson, Inc.
Used by permission. All rights reserved

Acknowledgements

A special thank you to the TTI leaders from around the world who contributed to this new edition: Fregy John, Dr. Moses Liancuh, Daniel Boro, Koudjoga Nenonene, Vu The Vinh, Dr. Jared Nelms, Sharwan Negi, Mario Kasih, David Anumod, Kevin Marsico, Joseph Mathai, Samuel Kabonaki, Andre Harriott, and special editor Lanie McKenna.

TTI gives special gratitude to Dr. Dale Hummel & Dr. Phil Largent for their investments in TTI leaders around the world. They have given permission to adapt and incorporate their training materials: "How to Lead the Church" and "Building the Inner Man." TTI is very grateful to Dr. Greg Kappas and Dr. Henry Oursler for their outstanding original work on Homiletics. We also appreciate Wyman Richardson, Glenn Lucke and Jared Wilson for their original contributions to Homiletics.

TTI also gives thanks to Dr. David Nelms, our Founder/President, for his vision and influence.

We thank TTI's Board of Directors who have given freedom and focus for the ministry. We are deeply moved by these men and women of God who serve as a base of financial and prayer partners that extend around the globe. These individuals, churches, ministries, networks, corporations, and organizations are essential and strategic to our collective health and Kingdom impact. Thank you!

We thank all of the TTI Continental Directors, National Directors, and other leaders for your ministry of love and commitment. You are the ones that forge into new frontiers with the Gospel. You truly are our heroes.

Finally, we are forever grateful to you, the church planter. You are planting an orchard, a church planting center, through your local church that will touch your region and the world with the Gospel of Jesus Christ. We are honored to serve the Lord Jesus Christ and you. You will make a difference for our great God as you multiply healthy churches for His glory. We love you and believe in you!

This workbook is the second of TTI's ten core workbooks which assist in equipping church planting leaders to start churches that saturate a region and help reach every man, woman, and child with the Good News of our Lord.

TTI Core Curriculum

Workbook Number/Course:

1. Discovering the Bible
2. **Communicating the Bible**
3. The Book of Acts & Church Planting Movements
4. Old Testament 1
5. Old Testament 2
6. New Testament Gospels
7. The Heart of the Church Planter (Pastoral Epistles)
8. New Testament General Letters
9. Major Bible Doctrines
10. Apologetics-Church History-Spiritual Warfare

Table of Contents

Section 1
Welcome & Introduction 5
Chapter 1: Communicating God's Word in Different Sized Groups ... 12

Section 2
Chapter 2: Basic Questions on Communications God's Word 24
Chapter 3: Hearing God's Voice 31

Section 3
Chapter 4: God's Calling to Communicate the Bible 40
Chapter 5: The Heart of the Communicator 47
Chapter 6: Learning to Communicate 51
Chapter 7: The Role of the Holy Spirit in Communication 56

Section 4
Chapter 8: The Big Idea & Application 61
Chapter 9: Introduction, Outline, Illustrations, & Conclusion 66
Chapter 10: The Communication Process 71
Chapter 11: Communication Skills 77

Section 5
Chapter 12: Warnings for Communicators.................................... 83
Chapter 13: Developing & Training Other Communicators 89
Appendix, Sermon Samples, & Additional Resources 93

Welcome & Introduction

Congratulations on finishing **Discovering the Bible** (Book 1)! To be called by God to make disciples and plant churches is one of the most exciting callings a person can have. As you grow in faithfulness and maturity, you will be required to learn to communicate the Bible well. This manual will help you develop this important skill.

The Apostle Paul wrote the following to Timothy near the end of his life:

"I charge you therefore before God and the Lord Jesus Christ, who will judge the living and the dead at His appearing and His kingdom: Preach the word! Be ready in season and out of season. Convince, rebuke, exhort, with all longsuffering and teaching. For the time will come when they will not endure sound doctrine, but according to their own desires, because they have itching ears, they will have for themselves teachers; and they will turn their ears away from the truth and be turned aside to fables. But you be watchful in all things, endure afflictions, do the work of an evangelist, fulfill your ministry. For I am already being poured out as a drink offering, and the time of my departure is at hand. I have fought the good fight, I have finished the race, I have kept the faith. Finally, there is laid up for me the crown of righteousness, which the Lord, the righteous Judge, will give to me on that Day, and not to me only but also to all who have loved His appearing" (2 Timothy 4:1-8).

Seven Observations from *2 Timothy 4:1-8:*

1. **Communicating the Word of God is Very Important**
   Paul began this passage by saying, *"I charge you before God and the Lord Jesus Christ" (4:1).* Communicating the Word of God is a serious matter. It was central to Timothy's calling as a pastor and church planter.

2. **We are to Communicate God's Word, not our Own Message**
   The Word of God is the foundation in building up disciples towards spiritual maturity. Faith comes by hearing the Word of God *(Romans 10:17)*.

3. **We are to be Ready**
   We must study, prepare, and work hard at communicating the Bible. Keep improving. Don't give up. Trust God to make you into a strong communicator. All skills require practice. If you don't practice, you won't get better.

4. **Correct Doctrine is Essential**
   Some will fall away from the faith, not wanting to accept correct doctrine, *"because they have itching ears" (2 Timothy 4:3)*. We must remain faithful to God. Our message must always be in accordance with the truth of the Word of God.

5. **We are to be Committed**
   We must be sober-minded and endure hardship to fulfill our ministry. There will be hard and discouraging times. Stay focused on the Lord Jesus Christ. Allow Him to encourage you as you communicate His Word.

6. **We are to Do the Work of an Evangelist**
   Our message must be focused on the Gospel, telling others about God's grace in Jesus' death for our sin and resurrection for our eternal life.

7. **Faithful Service to Jesus will be Rewarded**
   Paul talked about the *"crown of righteousness" (2 Timothy 4:8)*, which he anticipated receiving because of His faithful service to Jesus. We, too, are storing up treasures in Heaven. We must remain faithful!

Group Discussion
Read *2 Timothy 4:1-8* again and imagine God is speaking these words directly <u>to you.</u> Which of the seven observations were most meaningful to you? Why? Now take a few moments to pray, asking God to make you a faithful communicator of His Word.

Review from Book 1: Discovering the Bible

Before getting into Communicating the Bible, it is important to review the 7 Steps of **Group Discovery Bible Study**. As churches are being planted, this model is easy to follow when you gather together. Every gathering can follow the structure of **Looking Back, Looking Up, and Looking Forward** as you use this Bible study method.

Step 1: Read (or listen to) the week's portion of Scripture out loud while people follow along in their Bibles.

Step 2: Have someone else read (or play) the same passage out loud while the group listens.

Step 3: Ask someone else to retell the passage in their own words.

Step 4: Allow the group to correct or add any points they feel were left out by the person retelling what they heard.

Step 5: Use discovery questions to encourage the group to interact with the passage. For example:
- What captured your attention in this passage?
- What did you like about this passage?
- Did anything concern or bother you? Why?
- What does this passage tell us about God?
- What does this passage tell us about man?
- What does this passage say about living to please God?
- Is there a command to obey or an example to follow?
- Is there a principle to apply or sin to avoid?
- If there are people who don't yet know Christ in the group, ask: "Does anyone want to accept Christ?"

Step 6: Prayer & Commitment- Challenge the group to obey God's Word.
- Take a few minutes for everyone to pray silently, asking the Lord how He wants them to respond and what they should do in obedience this week because of God's Word.

- Ask the question: "Since we believe God's Word is true, what must we do or change in our lives to obey God?"
- Have each person share what they will do to obey the passage over the next week.
- Record their answers and lovingly hold one another accountable.

Step 7: Have the members of the group identify people they will share the passage with during the next week and have them write down their names. Close with a prayer of commitment.

Using the Group Discovery Bible Study when you gather together will give a clear purpose and measurable outcomes to every gathering. As new churches are being planted, we strongly encourage you to follow this model, especially as the size of the group is small, allowing everyone to interact.

Getting Started

Similar to every church gathering, every training should include looking back, looking up and looking forward.

1. **Looking Back** gives everyone a chance to share about and listen to what is happening in the field. It provides an opportunity for encouragement, celebration, and accountability. It also allows challenges to be identified, course corrections to be made, and progress to be measured. Finally, it provides a chance to connect back to the core values, mission, and vision of TTI.

2. **Looking Up** refuels our passion for loving God and others. Spending time in prayer and in God's Word provides nourishment to our souls and inspiration to continue moving forward. This offers a chance for each disciple maker to continue to learn and grow as Christ-like leaders. Ministry is fueled by our relationship with God. Ownership of the core values, mission, and vision will only happen if we remain connected in relationship with Jesus.

Hearing from God and responding to His word is the primary aim of looking up. After each lesson has been taught, allow some time for prayer and reflection for each person to identify exactly what God is calling them to do. A simple way to do this is to ask God to show you the areas of greater obedience He is calling you to.

3. **Looking Forward** offers a clear plan of action with timelines and expectations of what to do next. It is important that everyone has clarity regarding what needs to be done before the next training. These next steps are based on what each person hears from God and also the assignments listed in the training. There should be a strong commitment to following through and staying accountable throughout the process. Each trainer should make a note of the commitments made and hold all accountable.

Following the example of Looking Back, Looking Up, and Looking Forward will ensure that every training accomplishes the specific purposes, goals, and outcomes designed.

Chapter 1:
Trainers Guide

 **Look Back**

Give everyone a chance to share, hear from others, and be held accountable. Focus on encouragement, celebration, and following through with assignments.
- Discuss what each person has learned and has applied to their own life from Book 1: Discovering the Bible. How have they trained others?

 Look Up

This chapter introduces how to communicate God's Word in different sized groups. It is critical that you focus on the following as you train through this chapter:
- Review each group size and be sure everyone understands the role of every Paul, Timothy, and Titus. Identify the similarities and differences among the various group sizes.
- Make sure that everyone can apply the method of looking back, up, and forward to the Group Discovery Bible Study.

 Look Forward

Before reviewing the assignments for this chapter, pause and prayerfully discuss the following questions:
- How is God speaking to your heart today?
- How is God calling you to greater obedience?
- What will you do today & this week in response to God's voice?
- Am I clear on my role for each group size?
- How can I apply what I learned from this chapter into the gathering of new believers I am leading?

Assignments for this Chapter:

1. Based on the size of your newly planted church or gathering, try putting into practice what you learned this week. Report back on how it goes.

2. Continue sharing your story and God's story with 1 person from your prayer list every day. **Be sure to report back to your trainer what happens!**

Chapter 1:
Communicating God's Word in Different Sized Groups

As new churches are being planted, it is important for every Paul, Timothy, and Titus to be clear on the roles they each play as they look to move disciples and churches towards maturity and multiplication. Churches often begin as a result of new believers gathering together on a daily or regular basis for prayer, fellowship, encouragement, and Bible study. This happens in different locations, styles, and group sizes. Sometimes it happens intentionally, and other times it happens by accident. TTI's hope is that every church planter will be intentional and purposeful as they begin gathering disciples together. Regardless of the size of the group, it is important for every disciple (new or old) to regularly hear from God and faithfully respond in obedience.

As you begin to gather disciples together regularly, you will need to learn how to communicate God's Word in different sized groups. This chapter introduces three different group sizes and explains what TTI suggests is the best approach for each.
- Smaller groups consisting of 3-15 people
- Medium groups consisting of 16-50 people
- Larger groups consisting of 50+ people

There are similarities and differences among each of the three group sizes. For example, the role of the Paul, Timothy, and Titus will change depending upon the size of the group. As the group grows in size, so do the costs and the space required for meeting together. The amount of time you have when you gather and even what you do when you are together is directly connected to the size, space, and dynamics of the group. What works well in smaller groups may not work well in medium or larger groups. Consider carefully the similarities and differences so you can lead well!

*All suggestions are given as a guide to follow with what TTI feels is the best way to lead towards reproduction and multiplication of disciples and churches. Every partner has the freedom and flexibility to apply what they feel is the most appropriate method in their local setting.

Smaller Groups
3-15 People

General Observations from Groups of this Size:
- **Examples:** House Church, Fellowship, Prayer Group, Cottage Meeting, Preaching Point, Cell Group, Life Group.
- **Locations they Meet:** Houses, under trees, open air, under sheds, community center, coffee shops, any possible space to meet regularly.
- **Cost:** Normally there is no financial cost or rent associated with meeting in this size group.
- **Level of Formality:** Non-formal.
- **Sitting Style:** in a circle facing one another...sometimes in chairs, on the floor, or on a mat.

Role of Paul: Assisting and Watching Timothy.
- Since the Timothy is the planter of the group, the Paul serves as the primary encourager for the Timothy, intentionally mentoring, coaching, and empowering him.

Role of Timothy: Leading the Church and Modeling for Titus.
- The Timothy is the planter of this group and serves as the primary leader, teacher, shepherd, and disciple maker.

Role of Titus: Learning and Assisting Timothy.
- The Titus is both a disciple and a disciple maker, assisting the Timothy and actively participating in the church.
- ***As Tituses are planting churches, the Timothy can take the role of Paul, and the Titus can take the role of Timothy.**

Suggestions for what to do when you gather:
This gathering size is very relational, and it is easy for all the believers to know one another. It is easy for each person to be heard and be held accountable. It is recommended to follow a Group Discovery Bible Study approach as taught in Book 1 and as reviewed above.

Model for Smaller Groups:

 ## Look Back

- Welcome any new people and appreciate them for joining.
- Give everyone a chance to share how God is at work in and through their lives, hear from one another, and be held accountable. **Focus on encouragement, celebration, and following through with commitments.**
- Summarize the key points learned from the previous gathering and tell how you applied them to your life and shared them with others.

 ## Look Up

- Spend intentional time in worship, prayer, and fellowship.
- Do a Group Discovery Bible Study. Encourage everyone's participation (even new people and children).
- Observe the ordinances (Baptism & Communion).
- Give an opportunity for sacrificial giving.

 ## Look Forward

- Before you look forward, pause for a moment in prayer and ask some of the following questions:
  - How is God speaking to your heart today?
  - How is God calling you to greater obedience?
  - What will you do today & this week in response to God's voice?
- Based on what was learned from the Bible study and how everyone is hearing God's voice, identify action steps for the week:
  - Encourage each person to share what they plan to do (I Will...)
  - Encourage everyone to share the love of Christ to the lost world.
  - Identify ways you can meet the needs of the people in the group as well as outside the group.

Moving from Smaller Groups to Medium Groups

As a young church grows bigger, the ability to sit together and hear from one another becomes increasingly more challenging. Hearing from each person and providing an opportunity to share and be held accountable is critical. However, it may no longer be realistic for everyone to have enough time to share as the group grows beyond 15 people.

Remember, **everyone can hear from God directly**. Consider breaking up into 2-3 groups when looking back and looking forward (one group for men, one for women, and another for youth/children, as an example). Be careful to avoid the trap of some people coming and going without ever being held accountable. Holding one another accountable is one of the most loving things we can do for one another. It should be done out of a genuine desire that others may know the Lord more deeply and may experience the joy and fulfillment of living life abundantly, being conformed to the image of Christ *(Ephesians 4:13)*.

For those leading a growing church, it will be important to look for those faithful and available disciples who are willing and able to take on more responsibilities with follow-up and discipling efforts. **Invest most heavily in those who are faithful in applying and passing on what they learn.** As the group grows, you may need to consider meeting in another location or meeting in multiple locations based on where people are living.

For a new location, you may consider choosing a new place where there is no church, the home of one of your Tituses (2nd Generation Disciple Maker), or another place. If you choose to start meeting in an additional place, encourage your Titus to take responsibility over the new group.

Medium Groups
16-50 People

General Observations from Groups of this Size:
- **Examples:** Church, House Church, Fellowship, etc.
- **Locations they Meet:** Houses, under trees, open air, under sheds, community center, building, or any possible space to meet regularly.
- **Cost:** None or minimal financial cost associated with meeting in this group size.
- **Level of Formality:** Non-formal, Semi-formal, or formal.
- **Sitting Style:** in a circle facing one another, in rows, on chairs, on the floor, or on a mat.

Role of Paul: Watching and Encouraging Timothy.
- Since the Timothy is the planter of the group, the Paul takes a lesser role as the group grows larger. The Paul publicly reinforces the role of the Timothy as the primary leader and continues to encourage and empower their leadership.

Role of Timothy: Lead the church as they model and assist the Titus.
- The Timothy is the planter of this group and serves as the primary leader, teacher, shepherd, and disciple maker. The Titus is given intentional opportunities to help lead the group (leading the discovery Bible study, prayer/worship, etc).

Role of Titus: Learning and Assisting Timothy.
- The Titus is given more opportunities to serve in the church in a variety of roles. They will begin to be challenged to consider what it would take to start additional groups.
- ***As Tituses are planting churches, the Timothy can take the role of Paul, and the Titus take the role of Timothy.**

Suggestions for what to do when you gather:
This gathering size is still very relational, and the believers generally all know one another. However, without being very

intentional, it will become increasingly more difficult for each person to be heard and be held accountable. As the group grows, it will be critical to intentionally develop leaders and plan for the next steps. By the time the place of worship becomes full, the Timothy and Tituses as a team should have a plan to plant a 2nd generation church in a new place…or identify a larger place to meet.

It is recommended to follow a Group Discovery Bible Study approach as taught in Book 1 by dividing into smaller groups led by the Timothy & Tituses.

Model for Medium Groups:

Look Back

- Welcome any new people and appreciate them for joining.
- Break up into smaller groups in order to give everyone a chance to share how God is at work in and through their lives, hear from one another, and be held accountable. **Focus on encouragement, celebration, and following through with commitments.**
- Summarize the key points learned from the previous gathering and tell how you applied them to your life and shared them with others.

Look Up

- Come back together as a larger group and spend intentional time in worship, prayer, and fellowship.
- Observe the ordinances (Baptism & Communion).
- Give an opportunity for sacrificial giving.
- Divide back into smaller groups and do a Group Discovery Bible Study. Encourage everyone's participation (even new people and children).

 **Look Forward**

- Before looking forward, pause for a moment in prayer and ask some of the following questions:
  - How is God speaking to your heart today?
  - How is God calling you to greater obedience?
  - What will you do today & this week in response to God's voice?
- Based on what was learned from the Bible study and how everyone is hearing God's voice, identify action steps for the week:
  - Encourage each person to share what they plan to do (I Will...)
  - Encourage everyone to share the love of Christ to the lost world.
  - Identify ways you can meet the needs of the people in the church as well as outside the church.

Moving from Medium Groups to Larger Groups

If a church grows beyond 50 people, the dynamics of the group will quickly change. **Resist the tendency to begin looking inward only and continue to look outward towards reaching new disciples.** There will be more formality and clearer expectations on: when people come, when to start, when to meet, what is supposed to do what, etc. All of these details should be planned clearly. It is possible that the believers in the church will be able to support the church planter financially and perhaps will even be able to purchase land, construct a more permanent meeting space, etc. Keep in mind there are positives and negatives associated with any decision like this, and all decisions should be done according to local context and resources. **Remember: Church is not a building but the body of Christ.** (TTI does not financially contribute towards buildings but invests in leaders and disciple makers).

Larger Groups
50+ People

General Observations from Groups of this Size:
- **Examples:** Church, fellowship.
- **Locations they Meet**: Under trees, in an open space, under sheds, in a community center, in a building, or in any possible space to meet regularly.
- **Cost:** Minimal or significant financial cost.
- **Level of Formality**: Semi-formal or formal.
- **Sitting Style:** In rows, on chairs, on the floor, or on mats.

Role of Paul: Empower and Commission Timothy.
- It is encouraged that the Paul publicly commissions the Timothy and the new church towards a great ministry impact and motivates them towards multiple generations of disciples and churches.

Role of Timothy: Lead the church towards maturity and multiplication.
- The Timothy is the planter of this group and serves as the primary equipper of the next generation of leaders (Titus & next generation). The focus should be on healthy reproduction and multiplication.

Role of Titus: Assisting and Leading.
- The Titus can lead in a variety of ways and roles. They are equipped and empowered to start their own group with 3rd generation disciples.
- ***As Tituses are planting churches, the Timothy can take the role of Paul, and the Titus take the role of Timothy.**

Suggestions for what to do when you gather:
Without being very intentional, it will become increasingly more difficult for each person to be heard and be held accountable. As the group grows, the Timothy must be very intentional with their Tituses to plan for the next steps. The Timothy and Tituses as a team should have a plan to plant 2nd and 3rd generation churches in areas with unreached people groups and in areas where there are no churches.

With a larger group, it may be more natural to begin teaching or preaching directly from the Word of God. As you grow and become comfortable with this, it will be a good method of communicating God's Word. *Note the rest of this book explains how to preach and teach effectively.

Remember: As you gather together in a larger group, do not lose the emphasis on disciple making and accountability to apply what one has learned and pass it on to the next generation.

Model for Larger Groups:

Look Back

- Welcome any new people and appreciate them for joining.
- Either break into smaller groups or consider having groups meet during the week so that everyone has a chance to share how God is at work in and through their lives, hear from one another, and be held accountable. **Focus on encouragement, celebration, and following through with commitments.** <u>If you do not keep the same expectations on accountability, people will likely drift away from taking personal responsibility to be a disciple maker. Make sure this does not happen!</u>
- Encourage a few people to share testimonies of how God is at work and how they are applying what they are learning. Remind everyone that the expectation is both to apply and to share with others.

Look Up

- Spend intentional time in worship, prayer, fellowship, and communicating God's Word by teaching or preaching.
- Observe the ordinances (Baptism & Communion).
- Give an opportunity for sacrificial giving.

 **Look Forward**

- Pause for a moment in prayer and ask some of the following questions:
    - How is God speaking to your heart today?
    - How is God calling you to greater obedience?
    - What will you do today & this week in response to God's voice?
- Reinforce that everyone has the ability to hear God's voice and encourage everyone to identify action steps for the week:
    - Encourage each person to share what they plan to do in their smaller groups (I Will…)
    - Encourage everyone to share the love of Christ to the lost world.
    - Identify ways you can meet the needs of the people in the church as well as outside the church.

 Group Discussion:
Review the 3 different group sizes introduced in this chapter and discuss how each person can implement these strategies into their own groups.

Assignments for this Chapter:

1. Based on the size of your newly planted church or gathering, try putting into practice what you learned this week. Report back on how it goes.

2. Continue sharing your story and God's story with 1 person from your prayer list every day. **Be sure to report back to your trainer what happens!**

Chapter 2:
Trainers Guide

 ## Look Back

Give everyone a chance to share, hear from others, and be held accountable. Focus on encouragement, celebration, and following through with assignments.
- Have <u>everyone</u> report back on how they followed through with what they said they would do since the last training. (This can be done as a large group or in smaller group.) Remember: Intentionally and lovingly hold those you train accountable.
- Remind everyone that training is for trainers. Are they training others with what they are learning?
- Review the similarities & differences in communicating God's Word in different sized groups.

 ## Look Up

This chapter answers some "Basic Questions on Communicating God's Word." It is critical that you focus on the following as you train through this chapter:
- **Remember to highlight the expected outcome and key principles!** Encourage memorization of key Scripture verses.
- Emphasize that everyone can communicate God's Word. Focus on the role of the Holy Spirit and the importance of focusing on Christ.
- **Hearing from God:** At the end of this chapter, allow for a time of silent prayer and reflection, specifically looking for what each person should do in response to God's speaking to their heart.

 **Look Forward**

Before reviewing the Assignments for this chapter, pause and prayerfully discuss the following questions:
- Am I able to communicate the Bible? How have I communicated it the wrong way? What areas need improvement?
- How can I grow in having Christ-centered communication?
- How is God speaking to your heart today?
- How is God calling you to greater obedience?
- What will you do today & this week in response to God's voice?

Assignments for this Chapter:

1. Do a Group Discovery Bible Study on one of three parables found in *Luke 15* (Lost Sheep: *1-7*, Lost Coin: *8-10*, Lost Son: *11-32*). (Note: Group Discovery Bible Study is explained in Book 1: Discovering the Bible, Chapter 1.)

2. Begin memorizing *Luke 15:10*.

3. Continue sharing your story and God's story with 1 person from your prayer list every day. **Be sure to report back to your trainer what happens!**

Chapter 2:
Basic Questions on Communicating God's Word

Expected Outcome: Every Disciple Maker/Church Planter will communicate the Word of God in a way that glorifies God, builds up the church, and spreads the Gospel to the ends of the earth.

Communicating the Bible is NOT about:
- Entertaining others
- Denomination or preferences
- Self-promotion or personal agenda
- Health & wealth
- Impressing or attacking others
- Culture or traditions
- Information alone

What Does It Mean to Communicate the Word of God?
Communicating the Word of God is about clearly presenting the timeless and inerrant truths of the Bible while relying on the empowerment of the Holy Spirit.

Communicating the Bible focuses on:
- Bringing Glory to God
- Jesus as King of kings and His Kingdom
- The Life, Death, and Resurrection of Jesus Christ
- Repentance, Eternal Life, and Life Transformation
- Equipping disciples for the work of ministry
- Growing together to maturity
- Strengthening faith
- Right doctrine and instruction for right living

Why communicate the Word of God?
We communicate the Word of God to bring the lost to Jesus and to produce genuine faith, true repentance, and real life-change in the hearts of those hearing the message. All of this is for the glory of God, the building up of the church, and the spreading of the Gospel to the ends of the earth.

How to communicate the Word of God?
We communicate the Word of God in a way that is most relevant to the listeners with passion, clarity, and truth, all with the empowerment of the Holy Spirit.

Who can communicate the Word of God?
Every follower of Christ can communicate the Word of God.

When should we communicate the Word of God?
Always. At all times we should look for an opportunity to communicate the Word of God.

Where should we communicate the Word of God?
Everywhere. Wherever you have a chance to share God's Word, you should.

Key Principle 1: We communicate the Word of God, wherever we are, whenever we can, to whomever will listen, in the most relevant way possible, with the empowerment of the Holy Spirit, being grounded in the Word, motivated and compelled by the love of Christ.

Remember: Each person brings their own unique personality and style to the way they communicate God's Word. Do not fall into the trap of trying to become others. Learn from others but develop your own style as a communicator.

Group Discussion: Have you ever communicated the Word of God to others? How did it go? Did you copy the style of others or were you confident in your own style? Have you considered that God has purposefully given you a unique personality and style of communication? Don't be afraid to be yourself; God can use anyone. Any skill requires hard work, practice, and patience.

Assignment for this week:
This week practice communicating God's Word in your fellowship group. Ask for helpful feedback.

It is <u>God's</u> truth that we proclaim.

"*For this reason we also thank God without ceasing, because when you received the word of God which you heard from us, you welcomed it not as the word of men, but as it is in truth, the word of God, which also effectively works in you*" *(1 Thessalonians 2:13)*.

God's Word is without error. Jesus said, *"Sanctify them by Your truth. Your word is truth" (John 17:17)*.

Biblical communication begins with a diligent study of the Scriptures. Paul told Timothy: "*Be diligent to present yourself approved to God, a worker who does not need to be ashamed, rightly dividing the word of truth" (2 Timothy 2:15)*.

The Role of the Holy Spirit
The Holy Spirit empowers and guides the speaker.
- The Holy Spirit is our comforter, helper, and aid *(John 14:16-17)*.
- The Holy Spirit fills and empowers us *(Ephesians 5:18)*.
- The Holy Spirit teaches us God's Word *(John 14:26)*.
- The Holy Spirit enlightens and convicts those who are listening *(Mark 4:9; John 16:13)*.
- The Holy Spirit convicts (charges as guilty) the world of sin, righteousness, and judgment *(Isaiah 6:1-7; John 16:8-11)*.
- The Holy Spirit glorifies God and enlightens His truth. *(John 16:14-15)*.

Hearing and obeying God's Word produces fruit. There will be genuine faith, true repentance, and life-change in the hearts of some who hear the message.
- When Nathan the prophet delivered God's message to King David, he repented and sought God's forgiveness *(Psalms 32, 51)*.
- When he heard God's message, Isaiah repented and declared himself ruined and undone *(Isaiah 6:5)*.
- When the Samaritan woman heard Jesus' words by the well, she repented, believed, and told the whole city about Jesus *(John 4)*.

- When the Thessalonians heard the Gospel, they received the Word with joy, turned from idols to God, and became examples to all believers *(1 Thessalonians 1:5-10)*.

The goal of communicating the Bible is life change. Unbelievers will come to faith in Jesus, and believers will respond with obedience to the Word of God.

 Key Principle 2: Communicating the Bible ultimately has three goals: to glorify God, to build up the body of Christ, and to spread the Gospel to the ends of the earth.

Our ultimate purpose in life is to glorify God *(1 Corinthians 10:31)*. *Isaiah 46:10* tells us that when God's Word is preached, His purposes will be accomplished. *Isaiah 55:11 says, "So shall My word be that goes forth from My mouth: it shall not return to Me void, but it shall accomplish what I please, and it shall prosper in the thing for which I sent it."*

True Biblical Communication
True Biblical communication comes directly from the Word of God and should be focused on Christ. The goal is to exalt Jesus *(Luke 24:27, 43-49)*.

- Christ-centered communication is centered on the cross (*1 Corinthians 1:18-25*).
  Every church planted must faithfully and effectively proclaim the Gospel message.

- Christ-centered communication humbles man and exalts Jesus (*1 Corinthians 1:26-31*).
  Jesus said when He is lifted up, He will draw all men to Himself *(John 12:32)*.

- Christ-centered communication must be sensitive to the culture without compromising the truth (*1 Corinthians 2:1-5*).
  You must know and understand the people and their culture. This is required to best relate the timeless truths of the Word of God to people in a way that they will understand. This is one of the reasons you must raise up future church planters from within the targeted

community. They are the ones who know their culture best. They are the ones who have contacts and relationships with people in their villages and towns.

- <u>Christ-centered communication cares for the listeners</u> *(1 Corinthians 4:14-15)*.
Church planters must care for the people in their church, community, and those not yet in the faith. They seek to love them, lead them to Christ, and help them grow to maturity in their faith and effectiveness in their service to Christ.

Assignments for this Chapter:

1. Do a Group Discovery Bible Study on one of three parables found in *Luke 15* (Lost Sheep: *1-7*, Lost Coin: *8-10*, Lost Son: *11-32*). (Note: Group Discovery Bible Study is explained in Book 1: Discovering the Bible, Chapter 1.)

2. Begin Memorizing *Luke 15:10*.

3. Continue sharing your story and God's story with 1 person from your prayer list every day. **Be sure to report back to your trainer what happens!**

Chapter 3:
Trainers Guide

 **Look Back**

Give everyone a chance to share, hear from others, and be held accountable. Focus on encouragement, celebration, and following through with assignments.
- Have <u>everyone</u> report back on how they followed through with what they said they would do since the last training. (This can be done as a large group or in smaller groups.) Remember: Intentionally and lovingly hold those you train accountable.
- Remind everyone that training is for trainers. Are they training others with what they are learning?
- Encourage a few people to share some of the experiences they had communicating God's Word since last week.

 Look Up

This chapter focuses on "Hearing God's Voice." It is critical that you focus on the following as you train through this chapter:
- **Remember to highlight the expected outcome and key principle!** Encourage memorization of key Scripture verses.
- God's Word is essential to hearing His voice.
- Spend extra time on the topic of prayer & fasting. Consider fasting together as a group in the next week.
- **Hearing from God:** At the end of this chapter, allow for a time of silent prayer and reflection, specifically looking for what each person should do in response to God's speaking to their heart.

 **Look Forward**

Before reviewing the Assignments for this chapter, pause and prayerfully discuss the following statements and questions:
- Spend time this week intentionally listening for God's voice. Make sure to respond in obedience.
- Try fasting one day or one meal this week.
- How is God speaking to your heart today?
- How is God calling you to greater obedience?
- What will you do today & this week in response to God's voice?

Assignments for this Chapter:

1. Keep a journal of all the ways God speaks to you this week. Share with your group what you heard and how you obeyed.

2. Begin Memorizing *2 Timothy 3:16-17* & *2 Peter 1:20-21.*

3. Continue sharing your story and God's story with 1 person from your prayer list every day. **Be sure to report back to your trainer what happens!**

Chapter 3:
Hearing God's Voice

Expected Outcome: Every Disciple Maker/Church Planter will hear God's voice daily by reading and meditating on His Word and will respond in obedience.

Hearing God's voice is a critical part of the Christian life. Do you know how God speaks to you? Do you recognize God's voice when He speaks to you in various ways?

God has revealed Himself and His will to His people for thousands of years. He still directs and speaks to us today *(2 Chronicles 36:15-16; Hebrews 1:1-4)*.

God communicates with us any way He chooses. He can even speak through a donkey if He chooses *(Numbers 22:28)*.

This chapter introduces seven ways God speaks to His children. **Primarily, God speaks to us through His Word.**

Regardless of how God chooses to speak, **whatever we believe God has said must be in harmony with the Bible. Even our Lord Jesus who was in full communication with the Father often said, "it is written"** *(Matthew 4:1-11)*.

 Group Discussion: A man with known family problems tells you God told him to divorce his wife. Read *Malachi 2:16* and discuss how to answer from God's Word.

Some matters are already settled in Scripture for all time. Therefore, we need to know what the Bible teaches. We must read (or listen to) all of God's Word to know what it says. We need to know what is in the 1,189 chapters of the Bible (If you read or listen to 3-4 chapters per day, you can complete the whole Bible in one year!). The best and only way to know God's will and voice is to read (or listen to) God's Word.

 **Key Principle: Read the Bible! Listen to it! Meditate on it! Memorize it! Obey it! Apply it! Communicate it!**

 **Group Discussion**: Do you have access to a Bible in your own language? Do you have access to a Bible in any language you understand? Www.Bible.is has the Bible translated in over 1,800 languages (both audio and written) available for free download. In the appendix of Disciples Making Disciples there is a Bible reading plan. How are you progressing?

Seven Ways God Speaks to His Children

1. The Bible

2 Timothy 3:16-17 says *"All Scripture is given by inspiration of God, and is profitable for <u>doctrine</u>, for <u>reproof</u>, for <u>correction</u>, for <u>instruction in righteousness</u>, that the man of God may be complete, <u>thoroughly equipped</u> for every good work."*

All Scripture is given by God: "*God-breathed.*"

"...knowing this first, that no prophecy of Scripture is of any private interpretation, for prophecy never came by the will of man, but holy men of God spoke as they were moved by the Holy Spirit" (2 Peter 1:20-21).

All Scripture is profitable or useful for equipping every believer for the work God has planned for him or her. The Scripture is profitable for four specific uses according to this verse:

- The Word of God gives us correct **doctrine to base our teaching on.** The Bible establishes what is right from God's point of view. God tells us what is right in His Word. As we move forward in our life, we often go the wrong way. We sin. The Word of God will rebuke us. We will learn from God's Word how we have drifted from God's way. Some people avoid the Bible because they don't want to face a rebuke from God.

- The Word of God **reproofs.** The Bible is living and active, challenging our thinking, behaviors, and values in order to bring them into line with God's ways.

- The Word of God **corrects**. God will use His Scripture to correct us. We can learn how to get back on the right path with God by **applying and obeying** Biblical truths. The word "*correction"* has to do with setting straight what is broken. Applying God's Word can set our life back straight with God! We need to use God's Word to teach people how to get back right with God and His ways.

- The Word of God is good for **instructing believers in righteousness**. This is referring to training Christ-followers how to walk right with God. The emphasis here is on how to do it. The Word tells us what is right and can train us in how to do what is right.

2. **Meditate on Scripture**

Psalms 1:2-3 says "*Blessed is the man ... his delight is in the law of the Lord, and in His law he meditates day and night. He shall be like a tree planted by the rivers of water, that brings forth its fruit in its season, whose leaf also shall not wither; and whatever he does shall prosper."*

We are to *delight* in the Word of God. As you prepare for a big feast, you delight as your eyes see the food before you. Do you delight in coming to God's Word? The Christian who delights in spending time in God's Word will be blessed for it.

Psalms 119:111 reads, "*Your testimonies I have taken as a heritage forever, for they are the rejoicing of my heart*." The delight increases as the Word so often brings rejoicing in our heart. Does your heart take joy as you read and reread the Bible (or listen to it)?

We also delight in what God says because we find the Scriptures so valuable. Consider *Psalms 19:10*, "*More to be desired are they than gold, yea, than much fine gold; sweeter also than honey and the honeycomb."*

Psalm 1:2 and *Joshua 1:8* explain the need of meditating on the Word of God day and night. To meditate is to fix our mind on or contemplate a verse or passage for a period of time. How often do you meditate on God's Word?

Colossians 3:16 says "*Let the word of Christ dwell in you richly in all wisdom, teaching and admonishing one another in psalms and hymns and spiritual songs, singing with grace in your hearts to the Lord."*

There are three results from *Psalm 1:3* that God proclaims will come to those who delight in and meditate on His Word. *He shall be like a tree planted by the rivers of water that:*
- *brings forth its fruit in its season,*
- *whose leaf also shall not wither, and*
- *whatever he does shall prosper.*

Your life will not dry up with a consistent, daily intake of God's Word. A spiritually dry life might be a sign of not meditating on God's Word as you should.

God also assures those in Christ who delight in and meditate day and night on His Word will prosper in accomplishing His purposes. **The word *"prosper"* means "to advance or push forward" in accomplishing God's will.** This one prospers because he is constantly taking in God's Word, remaining in communication with God and being able to follow His leading.

3. **Holy Spirit**

God speaks to His children through the Holy Spirit who lives in every believer. According to *John 14:26,* the Holy Spirit is our Helper, Teacher, and Reminder. *"But the Helper, the Holy Spirit, whom the Father will send in My name, He will teach you all things, and bring to your remembrance all things that I said to you."*

Jesus also identifies the Holy Spirit as the Spirit of Truth and our guide. *"I still have many things to say to you, but you cannot bear them now. However, when He, the Spirit of truth, has come, He will guide you into all truth; for He will not speak on His own authority, but whatever He hears He will speak; and He will tell you things to come. He will glorify Me, for He will take of what is Mine and declare it to you. All things that the Father has are Mine. Therefore, I said that He will take of Mine and declare it to you"* (John 16:12-15).

Group Discussion: How has the Holy Spirit led you to apply God's Word correctly? Satan as well as non-believers can quote Scripture correctly yet apply it incorrectly *(Luke 4:10-11; John 4:9-11)*. For Further study on this point, consider the following verses: *Acts 8:29, 10:19, 11:12; 1 Corinthians 2:4-5.*

4. **Prayer & Fasting**

Prayer is "talking" with God, "listening" to God, and "hearing" from God. When you pray, you should be authentic and sincere, just as the Bible records how Jesus "talked" with God and taught His disciples. To really know a person, you need to have regular contact with that person.

In the early church, the Apostles became very busy with many activities. However, Peter realized that those leading the church should give themselves "continually to prayer and the ministry of the Word" *(Acts 6:4)*. This clearly shows that prayer and communicating God's Word are inseparable. The effectiveness of the communicator depends on their dependency on God.

Fasting is a spiritual discipline of yielding ourselves to God and His purposes by denying ourselves the fulfillment of the natural desire for food. **Prayer with fasting is not a form of bribery or manipulation to get God to do something we want**. Rather, fasting with prayer puts us in a position to better hear what God is saying to us. There is not a command or guideline given in Scripture for how long a period to fast and pray.

Group Activity: There are numerous examples of prayer with fasting in the Bible. Break into small groups, let each group have a topic to study, and report back what is found.
- Self Denial *(Luke 9:23-24; 1 Corinthians 9:27).*
- Seeking the Lord's Protection *(Ezra 8:21, 23; 2 Chronicles 20:3-13; Matthew 4:1-11).*
- Conviction of Sinfulness *(Nehemiah 8, 9:1-3).*
- Brokenness over a Situation *(2 Samuel 12:16-23; Nehemiah 1:4-11).*
- Facing a Spiritual Breakthrough *(2 Samuel 5:17-20 and 1 Chronicles 14:10-11; Matthew 4:2; Mark 9:14-29).*
- Make a Decision *(Luke 6:12-13; Acts 13:1-2).*

- Increase Spiritual Sensitivity to God and what God is saying *(Mark 8:34-37)*.

5. **Body of Christ**

God speaks to us through other believers in the body of Christ. God can speak through a disciple maker to other disciple makers. Being connected to a local body of believers is important in order to grow in the Lord. **Whatever way God chooses to speak through others, it should always be in line with His written Word.**

"As iron sharpens iron, so a man sharpens the countenance of his friend" (Proverbs 27:17).

"Let the word of Christ dwell in you richly in all wisdom, <u>teaching and admonishing one another</u> in psalms and hymns and spiritual songs, singing with grace in your hearts to the Lord" (Colossians 3:16).

"Him we preach, warning every man and teaching every man in all wisdom, that we may present every man perfect in Christ Jesus" (Colossians 1:28).

For Further Study:

Biblical examples of God speaking to others through members of the body of Christ:			
Acts 6:3	Acts 14:23	Acts 16:10	Colossians 4:7-9
Acts 9:13-19	Acts 15:8-18	Acts 17:14-15	1 Thessalonians 1:6-7
Acts 10:28-29	Acts 15:35	Acts 21:4	Titus 2:1
Acts 13:1-3	Acts 16:1-4	Galatians 6:1	

6. **Circumstances**

Since God is sovereign over the circumstances of life, clearly God can speak to us through circumstances. *Proverbs 19:21* reads, *"There are many plans in a man's heart, nevertheless, the LORD's counsel – that will stand." Proverbs 21:1* states, *"The king's heart is in the hand of the LORD, like the rivers of water; He turns it wherever He wishes."*

God can work through the circumstances of family problems. In *Genesis 37*, ten of Jacob's sons angrily sold Joseph, their younger brother, into slavery. Joseph was taken by slave owners to Egypt. Egypt is where God wanted Joseph to use him in fulfilling His purposes for Israel's future.

God can speak through such a circumstance as in the life of the prophet Jonah. While attempting to flee from God's plan to preach repentance to the nation of Nineveh, he was tossed into the sea by the ship's crew and was swallowed by a huge fish – only later to be tossed by the fish onto dry land.

 Group Discussion: Are you facing any difficult circumstances right now? How are you handling them? What might God be saying to you? Or perhaps like Jonah, has God spoken to you and you have yet to obey? What step of obedience can you take today?

7. **Visions / Dreams**

Joel 2:28 says *"And it shall come to pass afterward that I will pour out My Spirit on all flesh; your sons and your daughters shall prophesy, your old men shall dream dreams, your young men shall see visions."* God may choose to grant to one of His children a dream or a vision as a means of speaking to them. **However, a dream or a vision can never take the place of God's written Word.**

<u>Assignments for this Chapter:</u>

1. Keep a journal of all the ways God speaks to you this week. Share with your group what you heard and how you obeyed.

2. Begin Memorizing *2 Timothy 3:16-17* & *2 Peter 1:20-21.*

3. Continue sharing your story and God's story with 1 person from your prayer list every day. **Be sure to report back to your trainer what happens!**

Chapter 4:
Trainers Guide

 **Look Back**

Give everyone a chance to share, hear from others, and be held accountable. Focus on encouragement, celebration, and following through with assignments.
- Have <u>everyone</u> report back on how they followed through with what they said they would do since the last training. (This can be done as a large group or in smaller groups.) Remember: Intentionally and lovingly hold those you train accountable.
- Remind everyone that training is for trainers. Are they training others with what they are learning?
- Encourage a few people to share some of the experiences they had communicating God's Word.
- Did anyone try fasting? If so, how did it go?
- How did each person hear God's voice? Did they respond in obedience? Explain.

 Look Up

This chapter focuses on "God's Calling to Communicate the Bible." It is critical that you focus on the following as you train through this chapter:
- **Remember to highlight the expected outcome and key principles!** Encourage memorization of key Scripture verses.
- Everyone has the ability to communicate God's Word. Encourage everyone by sharing one way God has gifted them and how they can use this gifting for God's glory.
- **Hearing from God:** At the end of this chapter, allow for a time of silent prayer and reflection, specifically looking for what each person should do in response to God's speaking to their heart.

 **Look Forward**

Before reviewing the Assignments for this chapter, pause and prayerfully discuss the following questions:
- How is God speaking to your heart today?
- How is God calling you to greater obedience?
- What will you do today & this week in response to God's voice?

Assignments for this Chapter:

1. There are a variety of ways we are to interact with God's Word. Try interacting with God's Word this week by doing each of the following:
   - Hear the Word – *2 Timothy 4:2.*
   - Read the Word – *2 Timothy 3:16-17.*
   - Study the Word – *2 Timothy 2:15.*
   - Memorize the Word – *John 15:16.*
   - Meditate on the Word – *Psalm 119.*
   - Obey and Apply the Word – *Ezra 7:10.*

2. Continue sharing your story and God's story with 1 person from your prayer list every day. **Be sure to report back to your trainer what happens!**

Chapter 4:
God's Calling to Communicate the Bible

Expected Outcome: Every Disciple Maker/Church Planter will obey God's calling as they interact with and communicate Scripture.

Although Timothy was a young disciple, Paul saw something in his life that made him believe Timothy would become a great leader, church planter, and pastor. He saw God's call on his life. Just because Timothy was young did not mean he was not qualified, gifted, and called by God.

"Let no one despise your youth, but be an example to the believers in word, in conduct, in love, in spirit, in faith, in purity" (1 Timothy 4:12).

Paul issued some very strong commands to young Timothy. As you consider these commands, reflect on the words seriously and apply them to your life.

"Do not neglect the gift that is in you, which was given to you by prophecy with the laying on of the hands of the eldership" (1 Timothy 4:14). The local elders had recognized and affirmed the calling that Timothy had received, and they publicly acknowledged him as a called servant of Jesus Christ. However, Paul knew that when Timothy was under pressure and hard times came in the ministry (as they always will), he would need to remember his calling and the ministry God had given him.

"Guard, through the Holy Spirit who dwells in us, the treasure which has been entrusted to you. Be diligent to present yourself approved to God, a worker who does not need to be ashamed, rightly dividing the word of truth" (2 Timothy 2:14-15). These verses tell us that even though Timothy was gifted, he would still have to work hard to fulfill his calling. Disciple making and church planting is challenging and demanding, yet it is a privilege. Effectively communicating God's Word is a difficult task, but the One who has called you is faithful *(1 Thessalonians 5:24).*

Consider what is involved in God's calling in our lives.

1. **What Does It Mean to Be Called by God?**
To be a disciple of Jesus is to be called by God, to God, and for God.
The expected outcome of being a disciple is to make disciples! We are called to be like Jesus and act like Jesus.

To be called by God means we are called into a relationship **with Him** and are called to minister **for Him**. This was true in the life of young Samuel. He grew in his relationship with the Lord, and the Lord's presence was with him. He also saw God use him in a mighty way in serving God throughout Israel *(1 Samuel 3:1-21)*.

Mark 3:14 tells us about Jesus' calling the disciples to follow Him: *"Then He appointed twelve, that they might be with Him and that He might send them out to preach."*

 Key Principle 1: We are called to be in relationship *with* Jesus and called to minister *for* Jesus.

John 15:16 records another similar statement by Jesus: *"You did not choose Me, but I chose you and appointed you that you should go and bear fruit, and that your fruit should remain, that whatever you ask the Father in My name He may give you."*

This statement was made right after Jesus described the priority of their relationship *with Him by abiding in Him.* To *"abide"* means "to remain" in relationship consistently. Just like the branch must remain attached to the vine and draw its nourishment from it, we must remain in a life-giving relationship with Jesus **every day of our lives.**

They were to bear fruit in their lives. The context tells us this fruit would be the changed lives of people they reached in their ministry, and so it is with us as disciple makers and church planters. The fruits of the Spirit in the lives of believers are listed in Galatians 5:22-23. **We want to see transformed lives and communities by reaching the lost and maturing disciple makers.**

2. **The Marks of God's Calling**
As disciples of Jesus, our primary calling is to be disciple makers. Additionally, God has uniquely gifted each disciple with specific giftings to assist them in accomplishing their primary calling.

   A. <u>A sincere love for Jesus and evidence of growth in Him:</u>
   Do you remember the story of Peter in *John 21*? He had denied Jesus three times before the night of His crucifixion. Instead of harshly rebuking him, Jesus restored Peter to Himself by asking the same question three times. Do you remember what it was? Jesus asked, *"Do you love Me?"* That was the heart of the issue.

   Those who serve Jesus must demonstrate a supreme love for Him. We don't serve out of obligation, fear, or duty. We serve Him because we love Him for who He is and for what He has done for us.

   Do you love Jesus? Are you growing in your relationship with Him every day? Explain.

   B. <u>A continuing passion to serve Jesus:</u>
   Do you have a continuing passion to serve Jesus? Do you love being used by Him in the lives of other people? Do you do it for His glory, or is your motivation to be noticed by others so that you will receive credit for yourself?

   C. <u>A giftedness to minister effectively:</u>
   You are called to be a disciple maker. Do you know what your spiritual gifts are? Are you developing those gifts and abilities to their fullest potential? By participating in this training and reading this manual, you are showing that you desire to grow in your effectiveness in ministry.

Key Principle 2: God has given the church gifted leaders to train others for effective ministry and to equip them for the works of ministry *(Ephesians 4:11-16).*

Group Discussion: As a leader in the church, how are you equipping others for the work of the ministry? Will they learn how to do the work of the ministry best by hearing or by doing? Review the chart "Disciple Making Goals" in *Disciples Making Disciples,* Chapter 14.

   D. <u>An ability to see the need:</u>
In *Isaiah 6,* the prophet feels broken by the reality of his sin. He cries out to God for forgiveness and cleansing, which he receives by mercy and grace through faith. Then God issues a challenge. The message of the Gospel needs to be proclaimed throughout Israel. "*Who will go for Us? Whom can we send?*" God asks. Isaiah responds immediately, *"Here am I. Send me!"*

Isaiah immediately saw the need. Others around him saw the problem. But Isaiah, having just received a fresh touch from God, saw how God could use him as His instrument to bring healing, grace, and forgiveness to God's people.

Group Discussion: What is the need in your community and throughout your country? How many unreached or forgotten people groups are living in your area? How could God use you and the people you are ministering with to be instruments of His grace? What are the needs you can address?

   E. <u>God's calling is always affirmed by others:</u>
We need each other in the body of Christ. *1 Corinthians 12:12-27* tells us that God has designed the parts of the body to need each other. This happens one way, among other ways, in leadership development by mature and established leaders recognizing the gifts and callings in the lives of younger, developing leaders.

Paul said, "*Do not neglect the gift that is in you, which was given to you by prophecy with the laying on of the hands of the eldership" (1 Timothy 4:14).* The elders had recognized and affirmed the calling that Timothy had received, and they publicly acknowledged him as a called servant of Jesus Christ.

3. **Our Response to God's Voice**

James 4:17 says *"Therefore, to him who knows to do good and does not do it, to him it is sin."* If you know what to do and fail to do it, even if you simply delay in doing it, James says it is sin.

Has God called you to do anything that you are not currently doing? Have you forgiven those who have sinned against you? Have you confessed your sins and set your mind on heavenly things? You are representing Jesus Christ, and any form of disobedience in your life will hinder your relationship with God as well as His work in and through you.

Assignments for this Chapter:

1. There are a variety of ways we are to interact with God's Word. Try interacting with God's Word this week by doing each of the following:
   - Hear the Word – *2 Timothy 4:2.*
   - Read the Word – *2 Timothy 3:16-17.*
   - Study the Word – *2 Timothy 2:15.*
   - Memorize the Word – *John 15:16.*
   - Meditate on the Word – *Psalm 119.*
   - Obey and Apply the Word – *Ezra 7:10.*

2. Continue sharing your story and God's story with 1 person from your prayer list every day. **Be sure to report back to your trainer what happens!**

Chapter 5:
Trainers Guide

 **Look Back**

Give everyone a chance to share, hear from others, and be held accountable. Focus on encouragement, celebration, and following through with assignments.
- Have <u>everyone</u> report back on how they followed through with what they said they would do since the last training. (This can be done as a large group or in smaller groups.) Remember: Intentionally and lovingly hold those you train accountable.
- Remind everyone that training is for trainers. Are they training others with what they are learning?
- Based on the key principle from Chapter 4, how did you help equip someone this week towards the works of ministry?
- Did you identify any specific needs in your community? How is God leading you to respond?

 Look Up

This chapter focuses on "The Heart of the Communicator." It is critical that you focus on the following as you train through this chapter:
- **Remember to highlight the expected outcome!** Encourage memorization of key Scripture verses.
- Seriously consider the 4 dangers of falling away from God. How is your heart?
- **Hearing from God:** At the end of this chapter, allow for a time of silent prayer and reflection, specifically looking for what each person should do in response to God's speaking to their heart.

 **Look Forward**

Before reviewing the Assignments for this chapter, pause and prayerfully discuss the following questions:
- How is God speaking to your heart today?
- How is God calling you to greater obedience?
- What will you do today & this week in response to God's voice?

<u>**Assignments for this Chapter:**</u>

1. Begin Memorizing *Psalm 73:25-28.*

2. Continue sharing your story and God's story with 1 person from your prayer list every day. **Be sure to report back to your trainer what happens!**

Chapter 5:
The Heart of the Communicator

Expected Outcome: Every Disciple Maker/Church Planter will do a self-evaluation of their heart to make sure they have not drifted from their love of Christ.

How is your heart? To whom does it belong?

2 Chronicles 16:9 says, *"For the eyes of the Lord run to and fro throughout the whole earth to show Himself strong on behalf of those whose heart is loyal to Him."* In other words, the Lord is looking for those whose hearts are completely His.

Four Dangers that can cause us to fall away from God:

Danger 1: Pursuing Head-Knowledge Instead of Heart-Knowledge.

Has Bible study become only a head-knowledge exercise for you? Head-knowledge means only thinking about something without putting it into practice. It means knowing but not doing. It is not wrong to study the Bible, but many people stop at the point of "head-knowledge" and never make it to the point of "heart-knowledge."

That was the problem with the Pharisees in the first century. Jesus told these scholars that they were mistaken because they did not understand the Scriptures or the power of God *(Matthew 22:29).* They had memorized huge portions of the Old Testament, but they never applied it to their lives. **May that never be true of us!**

Danger 2: Busyness Rather Than True Devotion.

Church planting is challenging yet exciting. It requires a lot of time and energy. You will be stretched beyond your physical limitations with training leaders, evangelizing, meeting needs, serving people, and leading the church. The danger will be not making time to seek God. **It is your responsibility – right now – to commit to a specific daily time to seek the Lord.**

Group Activity: Read *Luke 10:38-42* and discuss the difference between Mary and Martha. Who does your life resemble the most: Mary or Martha? **Describe your relationship with God. How are you keeping it as your top priority?** Remember: Activities and ministry involvements should be the overflow of your relationship with God, not the reason for it.

Danger 3: Losing Your First Love.

Planting a church and seeing it multiply is amazing, but it is possible to do all the right "things" and still miss out on what is most important. This happened to the church at Ephesus. This church had a great beginning. It was strong in faith and love and was growing in hope *(Ephesians 1:15-18)*. It was mission-minded, planting other churches throughout the region. It held to correct doctrine and had an effective ministry. They persevered through many tough times. There was certainly a lot to celebrate about this church. However, they abandoned their first love in the process of these good "things." *(1 Corinthians 13:1-3)*.

Group Activity: Read *Revelation 2:2-4* and see how many positive qualities you can find from the church in Ephesus. Can you identify what was missing from all of their good activities? Are you doing all the right things, but somehow your heart has grown cold toward Jesus? Have you drifted from your first love and become distracted by other things? Spend some time in prayer and reflection.

Jesus said three things to this church:
- <u>Remember:</u> the way it used to be when you loved Me with all your heart.
- <u>Repent:</u> confess your sin and turn back to God.
- <u>Return:</u> do the things you did at first. Return to the basics of your relationship with God. Seek God. Pray sincerely. Confess sin. Read the Word. Focus on Him.

Danger 4: Falling into Temptation.

1 Corinthians 10:12 is a great word to disciple makers/church planters: *"Therefore let him who thinks he stands take heed lest he fall."*
We can begin to think we are so strong that we could not possibly fall. A temptation is anything which seeks to persuade a Christian to sin against the Lord. The goal of every temptation is to cause an individual or group to sin against God.

1 Corinthians 10:13 gives us hope and perspective: *"No temptation has overtaken you except such as is common to man; but God is faithful who will not allow you to be tempted beyond what you are able; but with the temptation will also make the way of escape, that you may be able to bear it."*

The truth about temptation from *1 Corinthians 10:12-13:*

1. **You are in dangerous territory when you think you can't fall.** Watch out and be on the alert.
2. Temptations seek to overtake you but are not unique to you. They are common to everyone.
3. God never abandons you in temptations. He is faithful. See also *Psalm 33:4, Psalm 145:13,* and *Lamentations 3:19-23.*
4. God never permits any temptation to go beyond what you are able to endure. He said: *"My grace is sufficient for you, for My strength is made perfect in weakness" (2 Corinthians 12:9).*
5. God always makes a way of escape so that you can endure every temptation.

As a disciple maker/church planter, you will be tempted more times than you could count. Satan will seek to destroy your ministry, your marriage, your character, and your testimony like a thief *(John 10:10).* You must remain strong and alert.

<u>**Assignments for this Chapter:**</u>

1. Begin Memorizing *Psalm 73:25-28.*

2. Continue sharing your story and God's story with 1 person from your prayer list every day. **Be sure to report back to your trainer what happens!**

Chapter 6:
Trainers Guide

 Look Back

Give everyone a chance to share, hear from others, and be held accountable. Focus on encouragement, celebration, and following through with assignments.
- Have <u>everyone</u> report back on how they followed through with what they said they would do since the last training. (This can be done as a large group or in smaller groups.) Remember: Intentionally and lovingly hold those you train accountable.
- Remind everyone that training is for trainers. Are they training others with what they are learning?

 Look Up

This chapter focuses on sharing "Learning to Communicate." It is critical that you focus on the following as you train through this chapter:
- **Remember to highlight the expected outcome and key principles!** Encourage memorization of key Scripture verses.
- **Hearing from God:** At the end of this chapter, allow for a time of silent prayer and reflection, specifically looking for what each person should do in response to God's speaking to their heart.

 Look Forward

Before reviewing the Assignments for this chapter, pause and prayerfully discuss the following questions:
- How is God speaking to your heart today?
- How is God calling you to greater obedience?
- What will you do today & this week in response to God's voice?

Chapter 6:
Learning to Communicate

Expected Outcome: Every Disciple Maker/Church Planter will communicate God's Word with simplicity, addressing the needs and brokenness of listeners.

Jesus' Example:
At the conclusion of the Sermon on the Mount *(Matthew 5-7)*, "*the people were astonished at His teaching, for He taught them as one having authority, and not as the scribes*" (Matthew 7:28-29). *Matthew 22:33* records a similar response: "*And when the multitudes heard this, they were astonished at His teaching.*" They were very impressed, surprised, and delighted. *Mark 12:37* says, "*the common people heard Him gladly.*"

People enjoyed listening to Jesus preach and teach. They had never heard anyone speak to them the way Jesus did. They were captivated by His speaking.

To capture the attention of men and women like Jesus did, we must communicate spiritual truth the way He did: with clarity, passion, and authority. **Jesus must be our model.** In *John 12:49* Jesus said, "*I have not spoken on My own authority, but the Father who sent Me gave Me a command, what I should say and what I should speak.*"

There is so much to learn from Jesus' style of communication.

1. **Begin with People's Needs, Hurts, and Interests.**

Jesus often taught in response to a question or a problem from someone in the crowd. He was relevant, was to-the-point, and addressed the need.

Jesus had Good News to share, and people responded to it because He began where they were, in their needs, hurts, and interests. **Our message must be Good News (the gospel).**

A. By beginning with people's needs, you immediately gain the attention of those listening. Effective communicators understand and use this principle. Wise teachers know how to start with the students' interests and move them toward the main point.

B. Your audience should influence how you start your message. When Paul spoke to the group of philosophers in *Acts 17*, he addressed their interests and concerns (He even quoted several of their local philosophers). He ultimately directed the message toward the resurrection of Jesus, the message they needed to hear (the gospel).

Group Discussion: Notice in *Acts 17:16* that Paul was waiting for his friends to join him in Athens. He saw the need and took the opportunity to preach the Word of God. Can you share a time that you have done something like this in the past? Are there any opportunities in your local community you could take advantage of?

Key Principle 1: Regardless of where you are or how you begin communicating, always point people to Jesus.

2. **Relate Truth to Life.**

The deepest kind of teaching is that which makes a difference in people's daily lives. For example, Jesus told the Samaritan woman at the well that he had living water *(John 4).*

The Bible was not only given to increase our knowledge but to change our lives. The goal is Christ-like character.

Group Activity: Break into two groups. The first group will try to name 10 places that Jesus communicated from (a boat, hill, etc). The second group will try to name 10 objects that Jesus used to relate truth to life (a coin, bird, etc). Report your results. With this in mind, it is clear we can communicate God's Word wherever we are with whatever is available to us.

3. **Communicate in a Way that is Interesting.**

The crowds loved to listen to Jesus. *Mark 12:37* says: *"The common people heard Him gladly."* The term "common people" refers to the normal, uneducated, and untrained people of the day. They listened with delight when Jesus spoke.

 Key Principle 2: The goal of communication is transformation by the Word of God through the work of the Spirit of God.

Jesus captured large crowds' interests with techniques we can use:

A. **Jesus told stories to make a point.** Jesus was a master story-teller. He would state a point and then tell a parable to teach that truth. In fact, the Bible shows that story-telling was Jesus' most common technique when speaking to a crowd. *"All these things Jesus spoke to the multitude in parables; and without a parable He did not speak to them"* (Matthew 13:34).

B. **Jesus used simple language.** He spoke in terms that normal people could understand. He used the common language of His day and talked about birds, flowers, lost coins, and other everyday objects His listeners would know about.

Jesus taught deep truths in simple ways. Today we do the opposite. We teach simple truths in complicated ways, and the result is confusion, disinterest, and rejection. **When we preach, teach, and train like Jesus, we will increase the impact of His ministry.**

<u>Assignments for this Chapter:</u>

1. Do a Group Discovery Bible Study on one of Jesus' most famous teachings, The Sermon on the Mount, from *Matthew 5:1-7:28. (Matthew 5:1-12, 12-16, 43-48, 6:19-24).* Focus on starting with the identified needs and hurts of the community.

2. Like Jesus, use the surrounding context (including objects and places) to share the Gospel. Continue sharing your story and God's story with 1 person from your prayer list every day. **Be sure to report back to your trainer what happens!**

Chapter 7:
Trainers Guide

 **Look Back**

Give everyone a chance to share, hear from others, and be held accountable. Focus on encouragement, celebration, and following through with assignments.
- Have <u>everyone</u> report back on how they followed through with what they said they would do since the last training. (This can be done as a large group or in smaller groups.) Remember: Intentionally and lovingly hold those you train accountable.
- How did you apply what you learned about Jesus' communication style?
- Were you able to identify people's needs, hurts, and interests? Share your experiences with one another.
- Remind everyone that training is for trainers. Are they training others with what they are learning?

 Look Up

This chapter focuses on sharing "The Role of the Holy Spirit in Communication." It is critical that you focus on the following as you train through this chapter:
- **Remember to highlight the expected outcome and key principle!** Encourage memorization of key Scripture verses.
- **Hearing from God:** At the end of this chapter, allow for a time of silent prayer and reflection, specifically looking for what each person should do in response to God's speaking to their heart.
- Emphasize the importance of completely depending on the Holy Spirit when communicating the Bible.

 **Look Forward**

Before reviewing the Assignments for this chapter, pause and prayerfully discuss the following questions:
- How is God speaking to your heart today?
- How is God calling you to greater obedience?
- What will you do today & this week in response to God's voice?

Assignments for this Chapter:

1. Begin Memorizing *Galatians 5:22-23*.

2. Are you being sensitive to the way the Spirit of God is moving in the heart of the people on your list? What about people not on your list? Share your story and God's story with these people this week. **Be sure to report back to your trainer what happens!**

Chapter 7:
The Role of the Holy Spirit in Communication

Expected Outcome: Every Disciple Maker/Church Planter will depend upon the Holy Spirit as they communicate God's Word.

The Holy Spirit must be relied upon as we study and share God's Word. There are five primary roles that are involved when the Bible is being communicated: illuminating (making clear), guiding, empowering, convicting, and transforming.

The Role of the Holy Spirit in Relationship to the Speaker:

1. **As an Illuminator (Makes Clear).**

It is impossible to properly understand the Word of God apart from the Spirit of God making it clear. Illumination is not the same as revelation or inspiration. It is not concerned with communicating new divine truth but enabling us to **understand** God's truth in the Bible.

David prayed: *"Open my eyes, that I may see wondrous things from Your law" (Psalm 119:18).* That should be our daily prayer.

"Teach me, O Lord, the way of Your statutes, and I shall keep it to the end. Give me understanding, and I shall keep Your law. Indeed, I shall observe it with my whole heart" (Psalm 119:33-34).

Paul prayed *"that the God of our Lord Jesus Christ, the Father of glory, may give to you the spirit of wisdom and revelation in the knowledge of Him, the eyes of your understanding being enlightened; that you may know what is the hope of His calling, what are the riches of His inheritance in the saints" (Ephesians 1:17-18).*

2. **As a Guide.**

We must trust God to guide us in our preparation and in the communication process. Jesus taught that the Spirit would play a vital role in the life of each believer. In *John 7:37-39,* Jesus said, *"If anyone thirsts, let him come to Me and drink. He who believes in Me, as the Scripture has said, out of his heart will flow rivers of living water. But this He spoke concerning the Spirit, whom those believing in Him would receive."*

Jesus promised that the Spirit would teach the disciples all things and bring to their remembrance all that He said to them *(John 14:26)*. The Spirit would also guide the disciples into all truth, speaking not on His own initiative and authority, but only the words He heard from the Father and the Son *(John 16:13)*. We can trust Him to guide and direct us as much as we trust Jesus when He said: *"I am the Way, the Truth, and the Life" (John 14:6)*.

3. **As an Empowerer.**
Ephesians 5:18 says the Holy Spirit will fill and empower us for daily living and service. When Stephen preached, those in his audience *"were not able to resist the wisdom and the Spirit by which he spoke" (Acts 6:10)*.

Paul recognized that his speech and preaching *"was not with persuasive words of human wisdom, but in demonstration of the Spirit and of power"* (*1 Corinthians 2:4*). The power of the message was not in his own strength or wisdom but solely in the anointing of God. **We must rely on the Holy Spirit, asking Him to empower us and our message to change people's hearts.**

Key Principle: The Holy Spirit helps the communicator properly understand the Word of God, guides each spoken word, and empowers the message to change people's hearts.

Group Discussion: How are you dependent upon the Holy Spirit in your communication process? In which area do you need the most improvement?

The Role of the Holy Spirit in Relationship to the Listeners:

4. **As a Convictor (One Who Charges as Guilty).**
It is important to recognize that conviction comes from the Holy Spirit, not from the communicator. In *John 16:8-11* we see the Holy Spirit convicting the listeners of their need for Jesus, awareness of sin, God's righteousness, and the coming judgment.

Paul wrote in *1 Thessalonians 1:5, "For our gospel did not come to you in word only, but also in power, and in the Holy Spirit, and in much assurance."* The Spirit of God was at work as Paul and his companions preached the gospel. We can trust that men and women will come to faith in Christ as the Spirit of God works in their lives through the preaching of the gospel.

5. **As a Transformer.**

Transformation is possible when the Word of God is made clear by the Spirit of God.

"Now the Lord is the Spirit, and where the Spirit of the Lord is, there is liberty. But we all, with unveiled face, beholding as in a mirror the glory of the Lord, are being transformed into the same image from glory to glory, just as by the Spirit of the Lord" (2 Corinthians 3:17-18).

Paul knew that Christian growth was dependent on, initiated by, and empowered by the Spirit. He asked the Christians in the regions of Galatia: *"Are you so foolish? Having begun in the Spirit, are you now being made perfect by the flesh" (Galatians 3:3)?*

What is the result of the Spirit in our lives? *"But the fruit of the Spirit is love, joy, peace, longsuffering, kindness, goodness, faithfulness, gentleness, self-control. Against such there is no law" (Galatians 5:22-23).*

Assignments for this Chapter:

1. Begin Memorizing *Galatians 5:22-23*.

2. Are you being sensitive to the way the Spirit of God is moving in the heart of the people on your list? What about people not on your list? Share your story and God's story with these people this week. **Be sure to report back to your trainer what happens!**

Chapter 8:
Trainers Guide

 **Look Back**

Give everyone a chance to share, hear from others, and be held accountable. Focus on encouragement, celebration, and following through with assignments.
- Have <u>everyone</u> report back on how they followed through with what they said they would do since the last training. (This can be done as a large group or in smaller groups.) Remember: Intentionally and lovingly hold those you train accountable.
- Encourage each person to share how they were dependent upon the Holy Spirit as they communicated God's Word. How did it go?
- Remind everyone that training is for trainers. Are they training others with what they are learning?

 Look Up

This chapter focuses on sharing "The Big Idea & Application." It is critical that you focus on the following as you train through this chapter:
- **Remember to highlight the expected outcome and key principle!** Encourage memorization of key Scripture verses.
- **Hearing from God:** At the end of this chapter, allow for a time of silent prayer and reflection, specifically looking for what each person should do in response to God's speaking to their heart.
- Spend enough time in the group activity for everyone to understand the Big Idea and know how to find it in passages in the future.

 **Look Forward**

Before reviewing the Assignments for this chapter, pause and prayerfully discuss the following questions:
- How is God speaking to your heart today?
- How is God calling you to greater obedience?
- What will you do today & this week in response to God's voice?

<u>Assignments for this Chapter:</u>

1. Study *2 Corinthians 5:14-21*. Identify the Big Idea. Is it memorable? Does it adequately and accurately summarize the one thing you want people to remember? Do you have a clear application? Be prepared to share in your training center.

2. Continue sharing your story and God's story with 1 person from your prayer list every day. **Be sure to report back to your trainer what happens!**

Chapter 8:
The Big Idea & Application

Expected Outcome: Every Disciple Maker/Church Planter will communicate God's Word with the clarity of a Big Idea and a natural application.

One of the ways to help people remember is to focus your message around one Big Idea. A "Big Idea" is the central truth of a text which is both easy to remember and an accurate summary of the main point you want people to know, apply, and teach others.

The marks of a good Big Idea include:
- True to the central truth of the Biblical passage.
- People remember it and see how it relates to their lives.
- There is a clear path from knowledge to application and from application to teaching others.

1. **Big Ideas Should Be Biblical.**
   - Make sure the Big Idea accurately reflects the central truth of the passage and the larger context.
   - The Big Idea should be evident from the text.
   - Consider using the words of the text itself in the Big Idea.

2. **Big Ideas Should Be Memorable.**
   - Spend the time during your preparation to identify a Big Idea that is worth remembering.
   - Make it short and concise. You should be able to express the Big Idea in one clear phrase or sentence.
   - Repeat the Big Idea frequently throughout the message.
   - Encourage listeners to remember the Big Idea. You might even have them say it out loud with you.

3. **Big Ideas Should Be Significant.**
   - The Bible contains many life-changing "Big Ideas."
   - The Big Idea must have substance.

4. **Big Ideas Should Direct the Audience Towards Obedience, Application, and Teaching the Next Generation.**
   - What is God saying through this passage of Scripture?
   - How will this truth transform the lives of those who believe, accept, and apply it?
   - Why is it important to them, and why should they teach others?

How to find the Big Idea:
   - What does the passage say?
   - What does the passage mean?
   - What is the central point of the passage?

Once the Big Idea is found:
   - How should this concept be applied?
   - How can this idea be shared with others?

 Group Activity: Divide into a few groups. Let each group choose a passage from *John 4, 10,* and *15* and practice identifying the Big Ideas. Present your findings.

Develop an Application-Centered Mindset:

The goal of communicating God's Word is to see transformed lives, not just to share Biblical information.

David prayed in *Psalm 119:11*: *"Your word I have hidden in my heart, that I might not sin against You."*

As we learned in the Group Discovery Bible Study process, there are three key areas to consider when approaching the Bible. Reading God's Word, retelling God's Word in your own words, and identifying how to obey, apply, and train others. This is the ideal way to approach the Bible.

As churches grow, there is a natural tendency to introduce additional forms of communicating the Bible. Preaching and teaching are also effective ways that should follow the same pattern of reading God's Word, retelling it in the communicator's own words, and moving towards obedience, application, and teaching others.

Focus on Obedience & Application:
- **Be specific.** The words "more" and "less" are not specific enough. Instead of saying "I am going to pray more," you could say, "I am going to pray every day for 30 minutes for myself, my family, and my new church work." That is a specific application.
- **Be measurable.** Does it allow people to measure their progress?
- **Be attainable.** Suggest applications that are realistic.
- **Be relevant.** Does it apply to their lives?
- **Be time-bound.** Does the application motivate people to action and change with a sense of urgency?

 Key Principle: Your communication is most effective when your listeners have understood what the Bible says, are able to put it into practice, and teach others to do the same.

Do not assume people will naturally apply the Scripture to their own lives. As Biblical communicators, we must make extra effort in showing how the Word of God applies to life. If we are to be effective communicators, we must be application-oriented in our teaching and preaching.

<u>Assignments for this Chapter:</u>

1. Study *2 Corinthians 5:14-21*. Identify the Big Idea. Is it memorable? Does it adequately and accurately summarize the one thing you want people to remember? Do you have a clear application? Be prepared to share in your training center.

2. Continue sharing your story and God's story with 1 person from your prayer list every day. **Be sure to report back to your trainer what happens!**

Chapter 9:
Trainers Guide

 **Look Back**

Give everyone a chance to share, hear from others, and be held accountable. Focus on encouragement, celebration, and following through with assignments.
- Have <u>everyone</u> report back on how they followed through with what they said they would do since the last training. (This can be done as a large group or in smaller groups.) Remember: Intentionally and lovingly hold those you train accountable.
- Remind everyone that training is for trainers. Are they training others with what they are learning?
- How was communicating God's Word this week with a Big Idea and a clear application? Explain.

 Look Up

This chapter focuses on Introductions, Outlines, Illustrations, & Conclusions. It is critical that you focus on the following as you train through this chapter:
- **Remember to highlight the expected outcome and key principle!** Encourage memorization of key Scripture verses.
- Learning and practicing the ideas introduced in this chapter will help each person become a better communicator of God's Word. Focus on the concept of finding an itch and scratching it.
- **Hearing from God:** At the end of this chapter, allow for a time of silent prayer and reflection, specifically looking for what each person should do in response to God's speaking to their heart.

 **Look Forward**

Before reviewing the Assignments for this chapter, pause and prayerfully discuss the following questions:
- How is God speaking to your heart today?
- How is God calling you to greater obedience?
- What will you do today & this week in response to God's voice?

<u>**Assignments for this Chapter:**</u>

1. Practice preaching a message using the principles taught in this chapter. Find an itch and scratch it!

Chapter 9:
Introduction, Outline, Illustrations, & Conclusion

Expected Outcome: Every Disciple Maker/Church Planter will learn how to prepare messages with a captivating introduction, clear outline, helpful illustrations, and an application-oriented conclusion.

1. **Introduction.**
   The introduction is a very important part of the message and is sadly often overlooked. It should capture the listener's attention, introduce the subject, and motivate the audience to listen. You only have a few minutes to gain their attention and to get them to focus on the message.

2. **Outline.**
   There are many ways to outline a message. An outline not only helps the speaker to stay organized, but it also assists the listeners to follow more carefully. Make sure it is clear where the points come from in the Bible. Ensure there is a natural flow and progression to the message. **See the Appendix in this book for examples of Sermon Outlines.**

3. **Illustrations.**
   Illustrations are powerful tools that help listeners remember the contents of a message. People remember and respond to stories and illustrations. Illustrations have the ability to make connections and add feeling to a message or story. **Illustrations make the meaning clear** and keep people motivated to listen. Illustrations move the emotions. Stories, ideas, and visual pictures appeal to our emotions.

   Illustrations are like windows that let light into a room. Illustrations brighten our presentations and help people to see clearly what we are talking about. Remember, the illustration is to make the point of Scripture more understandable, not to become the main point itself.

4. **Conclusion.**
   A conclusion tells listeners when the message is about to end. It connects the main points and specifies a response which should lead towards obedience and application. For example:
   - Reinforcing something good: **I will keep** doing it.
   - Warning: **I will not** do it.
   - Motivation: **I will begin** doing it.
   - Stop: **I will stop** doing it.

Is your preaching good? Do not expect to be a great communicator as you begin preaching; it will take time and practice. A lot of preaching is uninteresting. It's boring. People yawn and daydream. They count the flies on the ceiling or constantly check the time on their watches or phones, hoping you will finish soon. **Preaching is not supposed to be that way.**

 Key Principle: Preaching should find an *itch* and *scratch* it.

When your body itches, you want to scratch it, right? Have you ever had an itch that you couldn't quite reach to scratch? It feels good when someone comes along and scratches it for you. The same is true of a message which contains both an itch and a scratch. **This is not the same as when "itching" refers to those who seek out false teachers to suit their own itching desires and turn away from the truth of God's Word** *(2 Timothy 4:3-4).*

This "itch" is when you bring up an issue your listeners struggle with, and this "scratch" is when you promise and then deliver the solution. Every message should present a problem that causes people to want to know the solution.

When you plan your message, look at the Bible story you are preparing to tell. Ask yourself, "What is the itch (the problem) and how does God scratch that itch (the solution He offers)? Let's practice delivering the *itch* and the *scratch*.

 **Group Activity:** Read the story of David & Goliath in *1 Samuel 17.* Identify the "itch" and the "scratch." Get your listeners to itch and want to scratch early by bringing up the problem right at the beginning of your message.

If you preach David and Goliath, and the itch is fear, you might begin by saying, "Everybody has giants in their lives. These giants may be sickness, death, poverty, what will happen to their children, loneliness, or many other fears." Elaborate on some common fears, and people will start to itch as you speak. They will want to scratch and will listen more carefully. They'll wonder, "When are they going to offer a solution to my fears?"

Next, read all or parts of *1 Samuel 17.* Talk about Goliath and how much Saul and the Israelites feared him. Point out that Goliath was their giant. Ask the listeners, "What are your giants?"
Call attention to the fact that David stepped onto the battlefield thinking the victory had already been won because he saw God as bigger than Goliath. State your belief that whatever giants we face, we must trust in God and let him slay those giants.

"Like David," you can add, "our faithfulness will become a testimony to everyone who watches our lives, and they will give glory to God." Preach like that, and people will listen.

However, never forget to always show your listeners Christ as their ultimate need and the passage's ultimate focus. In the story of David and Goliath, David represents Jesus Christ, God's chosen servant who would defeat that Mocker (sin or Satan) although it seemed impossible. The scared Israelites represent us, a people in desperate need of God to act for us through Jesus Christ. The greatest fear God defeated was the fear of dying apart from Him for eternity by resurrecting Jesus Christ from the dead.

Assignments for this Chapter:

1. Practice preaching a message using the principles taught in this chapter. Find an itch and scratch it! Show them Christ!

Chapter 10:
Trainers Guide

 **Look Back**

Give everyone a chance to share, hear from others, and be held accountable. Focus on encouragement, celebration, and following through with assignments.
- Have <u>everyone</u> report back on how they followed through with what they said they would do since the last training. (This can be done as a large group or in smaller groups.) Remember: Intentionally and lovingly hold those you train accountable.
- Remind everyone that training is for trainers. Are they training others with what they are learning?
- Share how you were able to preach a message this last week. Did you find an itch and scratch it? Did you show your listeners Christ from the Word of God?

 Look Up

This chapter focuses on "The Communication Process." It is critical that you focus on the following as you train through this chapter:
- **Remember to highlight the expected outcome and key principle!** Encourage memorization of key Scripture verses.
- As you focus on truth, passion, and clarity, give special attention to the seven stages of communication.
- **Hearing from God:** At the end of this chapter, allow for a time of silent prayer and reflection, specifically looking for what each person should do in response to God's speaking to their heart.

 **Look Forward**

Before reviewing the Assignments for this chapter, pause and prayerfully discuss the following questions:
- How is God speaking to your heart today?
- How is God calling you to greater obedience?
- What will you do today & this week in response to God's voice?

<u>Assignments for this Chapter:</u>

1. Prepare a message this week and come prepared to present your message to the entire group.

2. Begin Memorizing *1 Corinthians 2:4*.

3. Continue sharing your story and God's story with 1 person from your prayer list every day. **Be sure to report back to your trainer what happens!**

Chapter 10:
The Communication Process

Expected Outcome: Every Disciple Maker/Church Planter will communicate the Word of God with passion, truth, and clarity.

You are unique. There is no one in the entire world like you. From your fingerprints to the way you look, there is no one exactly like you. *Psalm 139:13-16* says that God formed our inward parts and knitted us together when we were still in our mother's womb.

God also has equipped you with spiritual gifts, a unique personality, passions, abilities, talents, and experiences that make you different from anyone else in the world.

One of the greatest temptations in ministry is to find people we admire and copy them. We reason that they are successful because of the way they do what they do, and if we want to serve God successfully, we have to do it that way. We copy someone who is successful instead of serving God in our own unique capacities. When it comes to the communication process, learn from others but be yourself.

Here are some suggestions to help you grow and mature in your communication abilities:
- Pray, Prepare, Plan, and Practice.
- Don't be afraid to fail because you certainly will.
- Seek out and accept critique, even it if is difficult to hear.
- Find out what does and does not work for you.
- Record yourself on audio or video. Listen to it, watch it, and see how you can improve.
- Ask people who are more experienced and more effective communicators to help you without copying them.

Group Activity: Break into groups of two or three and practice communicating a brief 5-minute message on the gospel. Encourage one another by graciously providing constructive feedback.

God uses us to communicate His message *(1 Peter 2:9).*
He has given us His perfect Word as completely reliable and without error. He also gives spiritual gifts, talents and desires, a passion to communicate, and open doors for effective ministry for His glory.

The way we communicate is important. We must give special attention not only to the words we say but how we present them to others. Our attitude, passion, behavior, sincerity, and delivery are each very important.

How should we Communicate?
- With passion, truth, and clarity.
- In a way that people will listen.
- In a simple way that relates to people.
- In a way that is more than just information.
- In dependence upon the Holy Spirit.
- With urgency while being focused on Christ.

Seven Stages of the Communication Process:

1. **Apply to Your Own Life First.**
   It begins with the speaker applying the message to his/her own life. As you apply the message to your own life, begin thinking through how to best communicate the Biblical truths. Practice, Practice, Practice!

2. **Choose the Right Words (Keep it Simple).**
   Once we apply the truth of the passage into our own lives, we begin to put those concepts into language that will communicate to our audience. The use of words is very important: keep your message simple, using words that your audience will understand. As you read through the Gospels, notice how Jesus communicated. He used words and images that His audience could relate with *(a farmer going out to sow seeds in the field, a lost coin, a wedding, or a widow asking a judge for justice).* In doing so, He was able to communicate deep truths to an audience who could relate and understand the points He was making.

3. **Deliver the Words Well.**
   - Speak clearly so people will understand you.
   - Speak loud enough so people will be able to hear you.
   - Be enthusiastic. You are sharing the greatest news ever!
   - Be clear in the organization of your message so people will be able to follow you.
   - Be yourself and do not try to be someone else.
   - When you stand before others, it is natural to feel nervous. As you practice more, you will become more comfortable.

4. **Anticipate and Try to Avoid Distractions.**
   As you speak, there will be distractions. Some distractions will come from the surrounding environment, such as a baby crying. Other distractions will come from people's individual lives. Spiritual distractions are Satan's attempts to confuse people's minds. He wants them to think about anything other than the truths of God's Word. This is where we must pray and ask God to stop Satan's distractions and to give clarity in the message so people will respond.

5. **Maintain your Listeners' Attention.**
   Some people love to listen when people talk while others do not; there are things we can both do and avoid to increase the effectiveness of our communication:
   - Problems can occur when we have too many points in our messages. Remember: keep it simple.
   - Problems can occur when we speak for too long.
   - Speak clearly and loudly.
   - Change the rate of your speech from fast to slow or from slow to fast.
   - Change the volume of your speaking voice from loud to soft or from soft to loud.
   - Use simple and short illustrations that will keep their attention and will help them remember the Big Idea.

6. **Listeners Accept the Message and Identify Ways to Apply.**
   At this point, your listeners will attempt to internalize the message into their lives. You will aid them in this process by using good illustrations and making clear points of application to their personal lives.

7. **Feedback.**
   The communication process is complete when you as a speaker receive feedback to your message. Feedback can occur in a variety of forms. It is critical for you to receive proper feedback. Consider questions like:
   - *What did you understand?*
   - *What was clear? What wasn't clear?*
   - *How can I do better next time?*

 Key Principle: The ultimate aim of communicating God's Word is for people to hear from God, respond in obedience, and apply what they learned to their lives in a way that results in transformation.

Assignments for this Chapter:

1. Prepare a message this week and come prepared to present your message to the entire group.

2. Begin Memorizing *1 Corinthians 2:4*.

3. Continue sharing your story and God's story with 1 person from your prayer list every day. **Be sure to report back to your trainer what happens!**

Chapter 11:
Trainers Guide

 **Look Back**

Give everyone a chance to share, hear from others, and be held accountable. Focus on encouragement, celebration, and following through with assignments.
- Have <u>everyone</u> report back on how they followed through with what they said they would do since the last training. (This can be done as a large group or in smaller groups.) Remember: Intentionally and lovingly hold those you train accountable.
- How did you apply the seven stages of the communication process this week?
- Remind everyone that training is for trainers. Are they training others with what they are learning?

 Look Up

This chapter focuses on developing "Communication Skills." It is critical that you focus on the following as you train through this chapter:
- **Remember to highlight the expected outcome and key principle!** Encourage memorization of key Scripture verses.
- Good communication makes a big impact when preaching. Carefully consider all the elements to delivering a clear and quality message.
- **Hearing from God:** At the end of this chapter, allow for a time of silent prayer and reflection, specifically looking for what each person should do in response to God's speaking to their heart.

 **Look Forward**

Before reviewing the Assignments for this chapter, pause and prayerfully discuss the following questions:
- How is God speaking to your heart today?
- How is God calling you to greater obedience?
- What will you do today & this week in response to God's voice?

Assignments for this Chapter:

1. You have just learned some basic communication skills in preaching. Pair in groups of two or three during the week and practice preaching a sermon. Evaluate your delivery skills with one another in the following areas: content, gestures, eye contact, facial expression, voice quality, posture, movement, and use of speaking notes.

2. Being Memorizing *2 Timothy 4:2.*

3. Continue sharing your story and God's story with 1 person from your prayer list every day. **Be sure to report back to your trainer what happens!**

Chapter 11:
Communication Skills

Expected Outcome: Every Disciple Maker/Church Planter will intentionally develop and strengthen their communication skills.

As you are communicating, is there anything that would create in others a desire to change? Without the Holy Spirit, none of this is possible. In general, the role of communicating God's Word is not to create followers of the preacher but followers of God. Do not look to get followers but to inspire leaders who will go and make disciples.

Approaches to Communication:

Some choices regarding style are neither right nor wrong. They are simply reflective of your personality. However, the first decision you must make is a value-oriented decision which relates to the way we approach the Word of God.

The goal when approaching the Bible is to understand the meaning of the Word of God. It is important that we not look to approach the Bible with an idea in mind and then look to prove a point. Rather we should look for the original meaning to understand what is being communicated.

 Key Principle: We should never use the Bible for our own agenda or to prove our opinions.

1. **Preaching through Books of the Bible.**
Choose a book of the Bible, outline it, and preach through it completely. Some books can be done in one setting, while others can take months or even years. There are benefits to this style:
    - You preach the whole Word of God without ignoring any sections. God delivered His truth to us in 66 books that had a unique purpose, context, and flow-of-thought. All of the Bible is profitable.
    - It enables you to cover each passage in its original context.

Remember to study through (or listen to) the entire book and apply it to your life before you begin to preach it.

2. **Topical Messages.**

Topical messages should be practical and focused toward specific needs or areas of instruction and can be very helpful to your audience.

There are times when it is appropriate to address or present specific topics. Perhaps it would be helpful to talk about what God says about marriage, parenting, spiritual gifts, the purpose of the church, or how to know God's will. Other times you might want to address specific topics like salvation, the nature of God, spiritual warfare, characters in the Bible, etc.

Remember never to make verses mean something that would be outside of the context they are placed in. Even the meaning of specific words depends on their usage in the sentence, not necessarily how they could be used in any case. Consider the immediate context with surrounding verses, the context within that chapter, the context within that book of the Bible, and the context within the whole Bible. The type of literature and the history will also give context to what a specific verse must mean.

3. **Evangelistic Sermons.**

All sermons should point towards Christ. Some can be specifically focused on a clear presentation of the Gospel for unbelievers.
- Evangelistic preaching has the specific goal of calling lost people to believe in Christ.
- It is God's desire that people come to Christ and receive salvation.
- Some passages naturally fit for evangelistic preaching. *Romans 10:9-10,* for example, provides a clear and passionate offer of the Gospel to lost people.

 **Group Activity:** Let each person prepare a 5-minute evangelistic message and practice sharing it in groups. Based on the feedback, make adjustments.

Assignment: Go and share the same message in your church this week and prayerfully consider where you can share this message in the next few weeks with a group of unbelievers.

What Difference Does Good Communication Make?

Good communication allows the Bible to be heard clearly and without any barriers. You should not be concerned about whether or not you are known as a great public speaker; rather you should be concerned that people understand and respond to God's Word.
- Good communication with bad content will lead people astray.
- Do not call attention to yourself but to the Word of God.
- The most effective speaking style is a conversational style that invites people to listen to you.
- If you are invited to preach for another church, do your best to offer an encouraging message to edify that body of believers.

There are multiple dimensions of communication: gestures, eye contact and facial expression, voice, and posture/movement.

Gestures.
The way a message is delivered is most effective when it appears natural. Many speakers are uncomfortable about body language during their presentations. The best way to overcome this is through practice. Ask others if you happen to do anything that is distracting while you speak. Do you repeat the same words? Do you rock back and forth? Do you look down for too long? Do you pause unnaturally? Adding gestures can add emphasis to our speaking and reinforce the message being made.
- <u>Descriptive gestures:</u> moving hands, jumping up and down, shaking head. Avoid doing things that might be seen as distracting to those listening.
- <u>Cultural gestures:</u> unique to each culture; they communicate a non-verbal message. Make sure to dress culturally appropriate depending on the church body.

Eye Contact and Facial Expressions.
Perhaps the most important delivery skill is eye contact. Look at people as you speak to them. Know your message so well that you

can concentrate on the people to whom you are speaking. Use appropriate facial expressions. Expressions are powerful! Be pleasant when you are speaking.

Voice Quality.
People sometimes have trouble pronouncing and articulating their words. Here are some helpful suggestions:
- Speak clearly enough to be heard by your listeners.
- Vary your rate (from fast to slow), your pitch (from high to low), and your volume (from loud to soft). Use pauses at key moments in your speech for emphasis.

Posture/Movement.
- Your posture can communicate confidence to your audience.
- Too much movement as a communicator can be distracting. Move when there is a purpose to do so and be sensitive to your surroundings.

Speaking with Notes.
Some people prefer to write everything they will say. Others prefer to write some basic notes and key words (outline). Others prefer to memorize everything they plan to say. You will have to find the way that works best for you. The main goal is that you prepare well and preach with confidence!

Assignments for this Chapter:

1. You have just learned some basic communication skills in preaching. Pair in groups of two or three during the week and practice preaching a sermon. Evaluate your delivery skills with one another in the following areas: Content, gestures, eye contact, facial expression, voice quality, posture, movement and use of speaking notes.

2. Being Memorizing *2 Timothy 4:2.*

3. Continue sharing your story and God's story with 1 person from your prayer list every day. **Be sure to report back to your trainer what happens!**

Chapter 12:
Trainers Guide

 **Look Back**

Give everyone a chance to share, hear from others, and be held accountable. Focus on encouragement, celebration, and following through with assignments.
- Have <u>everyone</u> report back on how they followed through with what they said they would do since the last training. (This can be done as a large group or in smaller groups.) Remember: Intentionally and lovingly hold those you train accountable.
- Share how you practiced preaching this week. What went well? What areas have room for improvement?
- Remind everyone that training is for trainers. Are they training others with what they are learning?

 Look Up

This chapter shares "Warnings for Communicators." It is critical that you focus on the following as you train through this chapter:
- **Remember to highlight the expected outcome and key principle!** Encourage memorization of key Scripture verses.
- **Hearing from God:** At the end of this chapter, allow for a time of silent prayer and reflection, specifically looking for what each person should do in response to God's speaking to their heart.
- Prayerfully consider the warnings in this chapter. Spend extra time in prayer and reflection.

 **Look Forward**

Before reviewing the Assignments for this chapter, pause and prayerfully discuss the following questions:
- How is God speaking to your heart today?
- How is God calling you to greater obedience?
- What will you do today & this week in response to God's voice?

Assignments for this Chapter:

1. This chapter contains advice for disciple makers/church planters. Prayerfully review and reflect on each point in this chapter. As you pray, evaluate your own soul, asking the Spirit of God to convict you of any sin, strengthen your commitment to Him, and give you boldness to model and proclaim the Gospel in your new church plant.

2. Begin Memorizing *1 John 1:9*.

3. Continue sharing your story and God's story with 1 person from your prayer list every day. **Be sure to report back to your trainer what happens!**

Chapter 12:
Warnings for Communicators

Expected Outcome: Every Disciple Maker/Church Planter will remain humble and will completely depend upon God as they communicate His Word for His Glory.

Warning 1: The Danger of Speaking for God.
The Apostle James tells his readers, *"Let not many of you become teachers, knowing that we shall receive a stricter judgment" (3:1).* As leaders and teachers of the Word of God, we are held to a higher standard and are subject to a stricter judgment, meaning we must approach the Bible with seriousness and humility.

You will be held responsible for what you preach and teach. Watch your doctrine closely. Approach the Bible seriously. Every day, remind yourself you are saved by grace and have the privilege of serving the Lord by communicating His Word.

Warning 2: Pride.
Standing up in front of people preaching the Word of God is a great honor. Sometimes people will praise your efforts and appreciate you in front of others. One of the greatest dangers for those who communicate God's Word is becoming arrogant.

- <u>The danger of pride:</u>
  "For all that is in the world – the lust of the flesh, the lust of the eyes, and the pride of life – is not of the Father but is of the world" (1 John 2:16).

  "Boast no more so very proudly, do not let arrogance come out of your mouth; for the Lord is a God of knowledge, and with Him actions are weighed" (1 Samuel 2:3).

- <u>The solution to pride- Be Humble and Give all the Glory to God</u>: *"But He gives more grace. Therefore He says: God resists the proud but gives grace to the humble...Humble yourselves in the sight of the Lord, and He will lift you up"* (James 4:6, 10).

Warning 3: Self-Sufficiency.
The more God uses us, the more grace He extends to us. However, it is easy for us to come to the conclusion that our success is connected to our own abilities and hard work. We must remember Jesus' words: *"Apart from Me you can do nothing"* (John 15:5).

 Key Principle: Apart from Christ, we can do nothing.

In the book of 2 Corinthians, Paul lays out his philosophy of ministry. He states the power of ministry comes not from *us* but from *God.* Paul writes,

> *"And we have such trust through Christ toward God. Not that we are sufficient of ourselves to think of anything as being from ourselves, but our sufficiency is from God, who also made us sufficient as ministers of the new covenant, not of the letter but of the Spirit; for the letter kills, but the Spirit gives life"* (2 Corinthians 3:4-6).

Warning 4: Losing Your First Love.
It is so easy to "look good" on the outside but to have cold and tired hearts on the inside. Here are a few suggestions to keep your relationship with Jesus at the center of your life:

- Don't tolerate sin in your life.
    - *Ephesians 4:27* tells us not to give the devil an opportunity in our lives. The word opportunity literally means a "place" or a "foothold." It is from there that Satan can use great influence.
    - Continually confess your sins to God *(1 John 1:9)* and to one another *(James 5:16).*
    - *Hebrews 12:15* cautions us not to allow a root of bitterness to grow in our lives.

- Guard your devotional and prayer times.
    - Make sure you are not studying the Word simply "to get a sermon." Study for your enrichment. *Love God with all your heart, soul, mind, and strength (Deuteronomy 6:5; Matthew 22:37).*

- Be accountable to others to make sure you are serving Jesus out of good motives. Be honest with them. Accountability is useless unless you open your heart and receive counsel and correction.

Warning 5: Loving the Praise of People.
God is the only One we can look to for affirmation and the statement *"Well done, good and faithful servant."* Avoid the temptation to start looking to people for their praise and affirmation. In *John 12:43,* Jesus scolded the Pharisees for *"loving the praise from men more than praise from God."* Remember our first core value: **It is all about the King and His Kingdom!**

<u>**Assignments for this Chapter:**</u>

1. This chapter contains advice for disciple makers/church planters. Prayerfully review and reflect on each point in this chapter. As you pray, evaluate your own soul, asking the Spirit of God to convict you of any sin, strengthen your commitment to Him, and give you boldness to model and proclaim the Gospel in your new church plant.

2. Begin Memorizing *1 John 1:9.*

3. Continue sharing your story and God's story with 1 person from your prayer list every day. **Be sure to report back to your trainer what happens!**

Chapter 13:
Trainers Guide

 **Look Back**

Give everyone a chance to share, hear from others, and be held accountable. Focus on encouragement, celebration, and following through with assignments.
- Have <u>everyone</u> report back on how they followed through with what they said they would do since the last training. (This can be done as a large group or in smaller groups.) Remember: Intentionally and lovingly hold those you train accountable.
- How did the warnings for communicators impact you? Did you do anything different this week in response?
- Remind everyone that training is for trainers. Are they training others with what they are learning?

 Look Up

This chapter focuses on "Developing and Training other Communicators." It is critical that you focus on the following as you train through this chapter:
- **Remember to highlight the expected outcome and key principle!** Encourage memorization of key Scripture verses.
- Developing the next generation of communicators will ensure the Word of God continues to spread to peoples who have yet to know the name of Jesus.
- Carefully discuss the practical questions for developing others.
- **Hearing from God:** At the end of this chapter, allow for a time of silent prayer and reflection, specifically looking for what each person should do in response to God's speaking to their heart.

 **Look Forward**

Before reviewing the Assignments for this chapter, pause and prayerfully discuss the following questions:
- How is God speaking to your heart today?
- How is God calling you to greater obedience?
- What will you do today & this week in response to God's voice?

Assignment for this Chapter:

1. If you have not already, pray that God will help you identify a few leaders in your growing church that you can begin intentionally training to be communicators of God's Word.

Chapter 13:
Developing & Training other Communicators

Expected Outcome: Every Disciple Maker/Church Planter will intentionally train and develop others to communicate God's Word.

Acts 13:1-3 (below) is directly relevant to church planters because it begins with the Holy Spirit directing the leaders of the church at Antioch to consecrate their best leaders for a missionary adventure of church planting.

> *"Now in the church that was at Antioch there were certain prophets and teachers: Barnabas, Simeon who was called Niger, Lucius of Cyrene, Manaen who had been brought up with Herod the Tetrarch, and Saul (who was later known as Paul). As they ministered to the Lord and fasted, the Holy Spirit said, 'Now separate to Me Barnabas and Saul for the work to which I have called them.' Then, having fasted and prayed and laid hands on them, they sent them away."*

What a teaching team they had in that church! These six men were great Bible teachers. What they were doing at Antioch was good, but God had greater plans to expand His Kingdom. It was exciting to think of what God was going to do, but it was hard for them to lose Barnabas and Saul.

Notice that they released them, prayed for them, laid hands on them, and sent them on their way.

You may be the only person trained to preach in your community.

 Key Principle: Part of your ministry is to find, develop, and train others to preach.

Reproducing Yourself:

2 Timothy 2:2 is the verse TTI has built its ministry on. The Timothy Initiative is named after this verse. It says, *"And the things that you have heard from me among many witnesses, commit these to faithful men who will be able to teach others also."*

In that one verse four generations of leaders are listed: **Paul, Timothy, faithful ones, and others.**

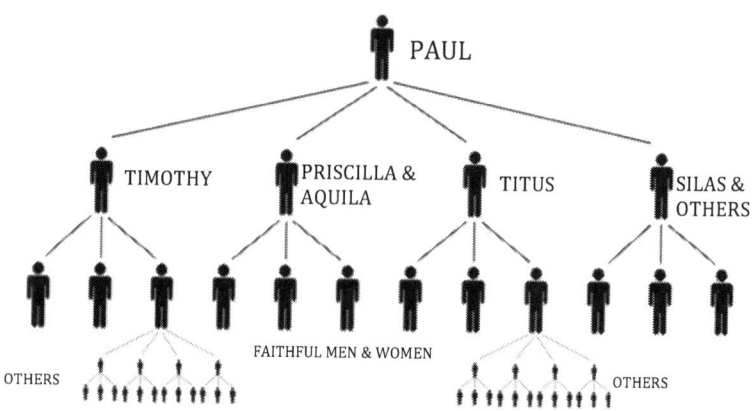

Think about that! Paul had built his life into Timothy (and dozens of others like Silas, Sosthenes, and Epaphroditus). Timothy was called to reproduce his life into "faithful men" who would grow as leaders and ultimately reproduce their lives into "others."

As one responsibility, you will need to train others to teach and preach. Just like you are being trained, you must also train others. Many of them will do very well. A few of them may even surpass you. That's great! As Barnabas freed up Paul to eventually pass him, you also should be secure in your own calling and abilities.

Develop a team of leaders and give them a chance to grow. The church will be encouraged to hear from multiple leaders with different gifts and abilities.

 **Group Discussion**: Who are you training to communicate God's Word? How are you training them? If they don't come from your ministry, where are they going to come from?

Remember TTI's development circle. As you watch your Paul or trainer, you learn. As you assist, you learn more. As you lead, you are developing others also. Just as your Paul helps you, you also help others too. Be very intentional to invite others into the process of watching, helping, and leading. Doing this will help develop a powerful team of leaders in the church.

Assignment for this Chapter:

1. If you have not already, pray that God will help you identify a few leaders in your growing church that you can begin intentionally training to be communicators of God's Word. Sit with your trainer sometime this week to discuss the questions on the next page.

Practical Questions to Discuss as You Develop Others:

- How can I prepare those who cannot read or write to lead a Bible study or even to preach?
- How often should I let others teach and preach? Should I focus more on developing people within the church or invite other pastors to the church?
  - Every time I let someone else preach, they do not do as well as I do. What should I do?
- When I preach, most people do not listen. What can I do?
- How long does it take you to prepare a sermon?
- How can I practice preaching my sermons before I preach them?
  - Typically, how long should I preach?
- How could I best handle distractions?
- What can I do if no one has a Bible?
- What do I do with those I am training who are learning and applying well but are not training others also?
- Are there any other questions that you or anyone else has asked?

Closing Words

Congratulations on completing *Book 2: Communicating the Bible!* While your communications skills can always be strengthened, you should feel more confident than ever when it comes to sharing the Word of God. As you have seen, communicating the Bible is a critical part of the disciple making and church planting process. Stay close to your Bible! Read or listen to it every day!

The next book in your training focuses on Church Planting by looking at the Book of Acts. It is going to be an exciting time as you study the rise and spread of the early church. Keep discovering the Bible daily and communicating His Word with truth, passion, and clarity. As you learn and apply things to your life, continue sharing with others all that God is teaching you.

Appendix 1
Sample Sermons

As discussed in this book, there are many ways to preach Biblical sermons. Consider these as examples to help generate ideas.

SERMON #1

This first sermon is an example of a topical sermon. The focus is the impact of Jesus' death on the cross.

Title: What Did Jesus' Death Accomplish?

Big Idea: Jesus' death was the full and final payment for the salvation of all who believe in Him (Jesus Paid it All)!

Passages: *Mark 10:45; Luke 9:51; John 19:30; Colossians 2:13-14; 1 John 2:1-2.*

Introduction:
Jesus was like a breath of fresh air among the religious leaders of His day (and of all time). He was unlike anyone else. He was unique and extraordinary in His life, but He was even more unique and extraordinary in His death.

Luke 9:51: "As the time approached for him to be taken up to heaven, Jesus resolutely set out for Jerusalem."

In dying, Jesus died the death of deaths – like none other.

1. **His Death Was A True Sacrifice.**

His death was the innocent for the guilty, the pure for the impure.

Mark 10:45: "For even the Son of Man did not come to be served, but to serve, and to give His life as a ransom for many."

This verse tells us Jesus' job description.

Jesus' death was fully of agony. *Hebrews 12:2: "Let us fix our eyes on Jesus, the author and perfecter of our faith, who for the joy set before Him endured the cross, scorning its shame, and sat down at the right hand of the throne of God."*

Matthew 27:46: "About the ninth hour Jesus cried out in a loud voice, 'Eloi, Eloi, lama sabachthani?' — which means, 'My God, my God, why have you forsaken me?'"

For the first time in eternity, the Son was separated from the Father. For the first time in eternity, the Father was separated from the Son. Why? For you and for me! God's justice was satisfied by Jesus' death on the cross.

2. **His Death Accomplished Our Salvation.**

1 John 2:1-2: "My dear children, I write this to you so that you will not sin. But if anybody does sin, we have one who speaks to the Father in our defense -- Jesus Christ, the Righteous One. He is the atoning sacrifice for our sins, and not only for ours but also for the sins of the whole world."

This verse tells us three things:
- His death not only made salvation possible, but it also accomplished salvation for us.
- We have an advocate in heaven, and we can stand against the accusations of Satan.
- His death atoned for our sins, once and for all.

If God did it, then it makes my salvation secure!

3. **His Death Was a Full Payment.**

John 19:30: "When he had received the drink, Jesus said, 'It is finished.' With that, he bowed his head and gave up His spirit."

Colossians 2:13-14: "When you were dead in your sins and in the uncircumcision of your sinful nature, God made you alive with Christ. He forgave us all our sins, having canceled the written code, with its regulations, that was against us and that stood opposed to us; He took it away, nailing it to the cross."

Conclusion:
What does Jesus' death mean for me? What does it mean for you? Because I have believed in Christ and have trusted Him as the payment for my sins, there are three specific truths that can be applied to my life:
- I am part of God's family.
- I am completely forgiven of my sin against God and am free from enduring the wrath of God for my sin.
- I have a new heart and a clean start.

In understanding that Jesus loves me, I also understand that he loves the world. Is there anyone I can share this message with?

There are many who do not know the love of Jesus and are outside the family of God. Prayerfully consider who God the Father might be drawing to Jesus.

Write down their names and find a time to speak with them this week.

Sermon #2

This second sermon is also an example of a topical sermon. The focus is understanding the Great Commission from the Biblical texts that mention it.

Title: "Jesus' Commands for Us" - A Fresh Look at the Great Commission in 5 Passages.

Passages: *Matthew 28:18-20; Mark 16:15; Luke 24:44-49; John 20:21; Acts 1:8.*

Big Idea: Go and Make Disciples.

Introduction
If you ask Christians to turn to *The Great Commission*, most of them will locate *Matthew 28:18-20;* however, that is only one of at least five times Jesus gave His disciples the command to go into all the world. This sermon shows the uniqueness of each of these commands.

A mission is a task we have been given to accomplish. A co-mission is a task we have been given to accomplish in partnership with someone else or a group of people.

Jesus is our partner in the *Great Commission.*

Ephesians 3:10 tells us that God's plan is to make known His manifold wisdom through the church. How will the world know of His manifold wisdom? By our following the Great Commission and going into all the world.

1. **We Are Sent –** *John 20:21.*
   - We serve the God who sends His people to all cultures in the world. Therefore, we must not only know God but also understand the cultures to which He is sending us.
   - The Great Commission is always accompanied by the presence of the Holy Spirit or the promise of His presence with us.

2. **To Everyone, Everywhere –** *Mark 16:15.*
   - We are sent to reach every man, woman, and child in the world.
   - We all have circles of influence in our lives made up of people we know, people we live nearby, our family and friends, and people we work with.
   - Churches also have circles of influence, and they are accountable to reach the people in those circles.
   - In Paul's ministry, he said to imitate him. Therefore, we should understand what Paul did.
   - In the book of Acts, he demonstrated many unique approaches to reach unique people groups. In Paul's ministry, there were different beginning points, but he always ended up at the same ending point: preaching the death and resurrection of Christ *(1 Corinthians 2:2).*

3. **With A Strategy –** *Matthew 28:18-20.*
   - Jesus said He has been given all authority in heaven and earth, implying that the Father gave this to Him.
   - He commanded us to make disciples. That is the primary verb in the Great Commission in *Matthew 28*. There are three words that qualify how we are to make disciples:
     - *Going.* This speaks of evangelism and telling others how they can know Jesus personally.
     - *Baptizing.* Baptism makes one's faith public and connects them to the larger body of Christ.
     - *Teaching to obey.* We are to teach new believers to obey all that Jesus commanded. As a result, they will become personally equipped and will begin to mature as a disciple.

4. **Telling a Message –** *Luke 24:44-49.*
   - The message we are to proclaim is the Gospel of repentance from sin and of faith in Jesus.
   - *"There is no other name under heaven given among men by which we must be saved"* (Acts 4:12; see also *2 Corinthians 5:18-20).*

5. **Empowered for the Task –** *Acts 1:8.*
   - How are believers equipped for this mission? The necessary tool is the empowering of the Holy Spirit.
   - We must be focused on the right things. *Acts 1:5-7* tells us the right thing is not prophecy and when Jesus will return but the mission He has given us. We must trust the work of the Holy Spirit in the lives of new believers, new pastors, and new churches.
   - We must be focused on the right places. Jesus talks about Jerusalem, Judea, Samaria, and the ends of the earth.

Conclusion:
We are sent to everyone, everywhere with a strategy, telling them the gospel message while being empowered by the Holy Spirit for the task.

Will you commit to this Great Commission? How are you part of fulfilling the Great Commission? Will your new church be committed to this Great Commission?

Appendix 2
Internet Resources

For those of you who have access to the Internet, below is a list of web sites that contain preaching resources and examples.

www.blb.org
www.desiringgod.org
www.executableoutlines.com
www.intothyword.org
www.lifechurch.tv
www.pastors.com
www.preachingsermons.logos.com
www.resurgence.com
www.saddlebackresources.com/en-US/Sermons/SermonsHome.htm
www.sermonindex.net/
www.sermons.logos.com
www.studylight.org
www.thegospelcoalition.org/resources
www.ttionline.org

Made in the USA
Columbia, SC
18 August 2021